Butterworths
Investigations

Butterworths Compliance Series

General Editor: Professor Barry AK Rider, LLB (Lond), MA (Cantab), PhD (Lond), PhD (Cantab), LLD (HC) (Penn State), LLD (HC) (UFS), Barrister

Series Editor: Graham Ritchie MA (Cantab), Solicitor

Other titles available in this series include:

Market Abuse and Insider Dealing Barry Rider, Lisa Linklater, Kern Alexander

Risk-based Compliance Tony Blunden, Andy Haynes, Stuart Bazley

Money Laundering Toby Graham, Evan Bell, Nick Elliott QC, Sue Thornhill

Investigations and Enforcement Dr Peter Johnstone, Richard Jones QC

Conflicts of Interest and Chinese Walls Dr Chizu Nakajima, Elizabeth Sheffield

Managed Funds Daniel Tunkel

Butterworths Compliance Series
Investigations and Enforcement

Dr Peter Johnstone BA, LLM, PhD
Reader in Law, University College Northampton

Richard Jones QC
Barrister

Butterworths
London
2001

United Kingdom	Butterworths Tolley, a Division of Reed Elsevier (UK) Ltd, Halsbury House, 35 Chancery Lane, LONDON, WC2A 1EL, and 4 Hill Street, EDINBURGH EH2 3JZ
Argentina	Abeledo Perrot, Jurisprudencia Argentina and Depalma, BUENOS AIRES
Australia	Butterworths, a Division of Reed International Books Australia Pty Ltd, CHATSWOOD, New South Wales
Austria	ARD Betriebsdienst and Verlag Orac, VIENNA
Canada	Butterworths Canada Ltd, MARKHAM, Ontario
Chile	Publitecsa and Conosur Ltda, SANTIAGO DE CHILE
Czech Republic	Orac sro, PRAGUE
France	Editions du Juris-Classeur SA, PARIS
Hong Kong	Butterworths Asia (Hong Kong), HONG KONG
Hungary	Hvg Orac, BUDAPEST
India	Butterworths India, NEW DELHI
Ireland	Butterworths (Ireland) Ltd, DUBLIN
Italy	Giuffré, MILAN
Malaysia	Malayan Law Journal Sdn Bhd, KUALA LUMPUR
New Zealand	Butterworths of New Zealand, WELLINGTON
Poland	Wydawnictwa Prawnicze PWN, WARSAW
Singapore	Butterworths Asia, SINGAPORE
South Africa	Butterworths Publishers (Pty) Ltd, DURBAN
Switzerland	Stämpfli Verlag AG, BERNE
USA	LexisNexis, DAYTON, Ohio

A CIP Catalogue record for this book is available from the British Library.

ISBN 0 406 932 514

Typeset by Columns Design Ltd, Reading, England
Printed and bound in Great Britain by Hobbs the Printers Ltd, Totton, Hampshire

Visit Butterworths LexisNexis *direct* at www.butterworths.com

Preface

This book is part of the Butterworths Compliance Series, a series which addresses many areas of law and practice in the field of financial services. It is written principally for compliance officers and those with similar responsibilities to give them an overall view of this complex area. Defining this area is not an easy task, and we have had to take a number of decisions regarding the inclusion and exclusion of materials. We hope that we have struck the right balance.

Only time will tell how the Financial Services Authority carries out its functions under the Financial Services and Markets Act 2000, and how the courts and tribunals will approach the detailed provisions of the Act. We hope that this book will, at the very least, provide assistance to those concerned with the important issues of investigation and enforcement.

The materials produced by the Financial Services Authority regarding their functions are many and varied and continue to emerge with frequency. We have done our best to ensure that the law is stated as at 14 September 2001. We would like to thank Darell Robinson of Barton College, Wilson, North Carolina for his assistance in producing the final draft.

Peter Johnstone
Richard Jones

September 2001

Contents

Acronyms

CJA 1988	Criminal Justice Act 1988
CJA 1993	Criminal Justice Act 1993
CJICA 1990	Criminal Justice (International Co-operation) Act 1990
DGFT	Director General of Fair Trading
DTI	Department of Trade and Industry
ECHR	European Convention on Human Rights
EEA	European Economic Area
EU	European Union
FSA	Financial Services Authority
FSMA 2000	Financial Services and Markets Act 2000
HRA 1998	Human Rights Act 1998
NCIS	National Criminal Intelligence Service
PACE 1984	Police and Criminal Evidence Act 1984
RIPO 2000	Regulation of Investigatory Powers Act 2000
SFO	Serious Fraud Office

Table of statutes

References in this table are to paragraph numbers

Table of statutory instruments

References in this table are to paragraph numbers

Table of cases

CHAPTER I

The Financial Services and Markets Act 2000: enforcement and investigations

Criminal offences and the role of the Financial Services Authority

1.1   Under the Financial Services and Markets Act 2000 ('FSMA 2000') the Financial Services Authority ('FSA') has the power to conduct investigations into a number of criminal offences. These can be usefully broken down into three categories:

- mainstream offences under the FSMA 2000 (for example market abuse);
- perimeter and connected offences under the FSMA 2000 (this would capture offences such as making false claims to be authorised or making false or misleading statements to induce investors); and
- those offences that the FSA can investigate, although the offences themselves are contained within legislation other than the FSMA 2000, for example insider dealing and money laundering.

Mainstream offences under the FSMA 2000

1.2   Under the FSMA 2000 the FSA may investigate a wide range of offences that are committed in England and Wales, Northern Ireland and Scotland. However, the power to prosecute is restricted to England and Wales and Northern Ireland. In respect of Scotland, prosecutions are brought by the Lord Advocate.

Market abuse

1.3   The introduction of this offence caused considerable discussion in both Houses of Parliament. The outcome of these debates remains, in the eyes of many commentators, unresolved[1]. One view is that the imposition of criminal sanctions automatically identifies this offence as criminal, and as such any person being investigated or prosecuted for this offence would be entitled to all of the protections afforded to suspects in any criminal matter. The position taken by the government was somewhat different, and a statement of compatibility with the European Convention on Human Rights has been issued. This effectively means that the government is satisfied that the provisions of the offence do not compromise human rights; and as far as the government is concerned the case for classifying this offence as criminal is not fully made.

1   The FSMA 2000, s 118 sets out the behaviour which amounts to market abuse. This section also confers on the Treasury the power to make orders that specify which markets and which investments are caught by this section. The section has proved to be highly controversial so far and a number of the issues raised are as yet unresolved, in particular whether or not the penal nature of the sanctions for market abuse will be found to be in contravention of the provisions of the Human Rights Act 1998. The basis of the section is that the provisions should supplement existing legislation, particularly in relation to insider dealing under the Criminal Justice Act 1993 and under the Code on Market Conduct. In addition, there is a specific attempt to prevent the use of misleading statements and practices as found under s 397 of the FSMA 2000.

Criminal behaviour

1.4   There are three offences relating to market abuse contained within s 397 of the FSMA 2000, but the behaviour that will constitute the offence is contained within s 118. The most important element is the definition of the term 'market abuse' which is to be found in sub-ss (1) and (2) of s 118.

1.5   There are three types of behaviour that are likely to be deemed criminal: first, behaviour that is based on inside information and is not available to the rest of the market; second, behaviour that will give a regular market user a false or misleading impression; and, third, behaviour that the regular market user is likely to view as behaviour that would distort the market.

1.6   The focus of the market abuse provisions is dealing with the effects of certain types of behaviour, and although these offences are criminal there is no mention of intention. It is therefore the case that it is not a requirement of proof that an offender is found to have intended the consequences of his actions, but only that a regular user would conclude that the behaviour amounted to market abuse.

Meaning of 'behaviour'

1.7   Before exploring each category under the market abuse provisions it is necessary to comment on the meaning of the term 'behaviour'. For the purposes of the FSMA 2000 behaviour that amounts to market abuse has four elements:

- the behaviour must be based on information, and the information that the participant holds must be one of the reasons for the behaviour (but it need not be the sole reason);

- the information must be information that is not generally available;
- the information must be likely to be regarded as relevant information by a regular market user; and
- the information must relate to matters that a regular market user would reasonably expect to be disclosed to other market users.

Use of information

1.8   In order that a judgement can be made about the use of information, it is necessary that compliance officers are able to determine what is meant by 'information not generally available'. The guidance notes do not specify what is not available, but rather what is meant by information that will be treated as being generally available. Information of this nature can be any, or all, of the following:

- information disclosed through an accepted channel for dissemination of information;
- information contained in records that are open to inspection by the public;
- information derived from materials available to the public;
- information obtained by observation;
- information available overseas which has not been made available to the UK public;
- information available to a section of the public; and
- information available on payment of a fee.

1.9   The FSMA 2000 is not seeking to deter the exploitation of information obtained through research or observation, and there is no bar to the use of information obtained due to the superior resources, expertise or competence of a market participant, particularly if the information obtained is widely available to the public (for example, by monitoring a public event).

1.10   The offences captured under Section 1 of the FSMA 2000 are actionable by the FSA and, in some instances, also by the Director General of Fair Trading. Many of the offences contained here are similar, but not identical, to offences contained in previous Acts; for example, market manipulation under the Financial Services Act 1986, making misleading statements under the same Act, and similar offences under the Banking Act 1987[1].

What is clear from recent prosecutions is that in cases of market abuse the FSA will be the lead authority[2].

---

1   Market manipulation under s 47 of the Financial Services Act 1986; making misleading statements as to insurance contracts under s 133 of the Financial Services Act 1986 and s 35 of the Banking Act 1987; making a statement, promise or forecast that is misleading, false or deceptive.
2   Eg, *R v Gangar* FSA/PN/108/2000 (14 August 2000, unreported).

Inside information

1.11 The type of conduct that the FSMA 2000 attempts to prevent can be broadly termed 'misuse of information'. The basis for this provision is that investment decisions are made on the basis of information that is available to all market participants on an equal basis. To trade on the basis of information that is not available to all may lead to distortion of the market, and such action is therefore a criminal offence under this Act.

Giving a false or misleading impression

1.12 It is reasonable for market users to expect that the information they receive is reliable; therefore any behaviour that is likely to create an inaccurate picture of the true market conditions will be treated as a criminal offence.

1.13 It is generally accepted that, at times, certain market users will have access to information that is not available to all market participants. Not all of this information will be relevant for the purposes of offences under the FSMA 2000, but some of it may well be; for example, trading on the basis of the information and, in doing so, realising a profit or avoiding a loss.

1.14 In the event that a person creates an artificial transaction, this may be held to be a criminal offence. The test that will be applied is whether the person knew, or could reasonably be expected to know, that the principal effect of the transaction would be to artificially inflate or depress the value of an investment. In order that the actions are determined as false and misleading there must be a real likelihood that they will have that effect, even if the likelihood is less than 50%. It will not be an offence if the regular user would consider that the principal reason for the transaction was a legitimate commercial rationale, notwithstanding the effect that the transaction had on the market.

1.15 What the provisions are seeking to distinguish here is the effect of the trading, for whilst it is accepted that the participant may have profited from their actions, the basic test that will be applied is: were the actions against the wider interests of the market?

Market distortion

1.16 This offence differs from that of giving a false impression in that in this case the behaviour is designed to impede the proper operation of the markets with the result that regular market users would view the interaction between supply and demand as having been distorted.

1.17   It is important for the purposes of compliance that market participants are aware of the implications of the term 'behaviour'. Behaviour includes action or inaction. It is therefore the case that to commit any one of the three offences outlined in para **000**, the participant must do or not do a specific act. However, culpability does not end there as, in addition, the behaviour must be such that a regular user of the market would be likely to regard the activity performed as of a standard that falls below that expected of a regular market user. A 'regular user' is defined as a 'reasonable person who regularly deals on the market in investments of the kind in question'. What this amounts to in legal terms is a hypothetical user, not a particular or actual user. There is no universal standard, and the FSA is clearly not seeking to introduce one.

1.18   For example, if commodity producer X is in possession of disclosable information which is relevant with respect to its shares, any trading in X's shares, either by the company, its staff or a third party, ahead of a general disclosure of the information would, in terms of the current draft Code, amount to market abuse. Moreover, any trading in commodity futures contracts to which the information is also relevant would also amount to market abuse. If, however, the information is not 'relevant information' in relation to the commodity futures contracts, trading in the commodity futures contracts would not amount to market abuse[1].

1   The example given is cited by the FSA in Consultation Paper 59 at p 22.

1.19   This can be taken further by assuming that the disclosable information in X's possession concerns a substantial reduction in the amount of the commodity that will be available to supply the market, and the effect of disclosing this would lead to the price being driven significantly higher (including in the futures market). In these circumstances it might be reasonable to expect X to hedge against any uncovered positions before they disclose the information; but the question to be decided may be whether it is reasonable for X to over-hedge in order that a subsequent profit can be made. It is argued that in the above scenario there is a balance to be struck between X gaining a competitive advantage and the actions of X disadvantaging the market as a whole. It is the view of the FSA that each case will be dealt with on its own merits.

The meaning of 'distortion': the distortion test

1.20   To be caught by these provisions the behaviour must be such that the regular market user would, or would be likely to, regard the behaviour as likely to distort the market. This is similar to the provisions detailed in para **000**, in respect of misleading statements, where again the threshold can be below 50% provided that the likelihood of a regular user believing that distortion is real and not just fanciful. Consideration will be given to the following factors:

5

- The more transparency there is on the part of the person building the position, the greater the opportunity there is for other participants to take action to safeguard their own interests. In circumstances of demonstrable transparency the market is unlikely to be distorted.
- Regular market users expect others to settle their obligations in order that regular users are not dependant on holders of long positions lending (unless inclined to do so).
- If the actions of a market user are likely to create a risk of settlement default by other market users then this may well constitute distortion of the market.
- Certain market behaviour will clearly give rise to a distortion, and the FSA sets out descriptions which include 'abusive squeezes', where a person has a significant influence over the supply of a product or expects others to deliver to him. He uses this position in order to distort prices for the settlement or to release from obligations to him.
- Price positioning, where a person enters into a transaction for the purpose of positioning the price of an investment or product at a distorted level determined by that person. This type of activity might typically include 'ramping' (driving up or down an investment price and then reversing the movement to realise a profit or avoid a loss).

This list is not exhaustive and it may be the case that the behaviour outlined above does not result in a distortion of the market. Conversely, there may be other behaviour that, by itself, would not appear to amount to a distortion but may be contributory or may act as an early indicator that there may be a distortion. The factors that would attract attention from the FSA as an indicator of behaviour that may lead to distortion might include price or rate movements significantly outside normal movement patterns, volumes of trades substantially outside the upper and lower scales average, backwardation (where futures prices are lower than cash prices), or where repo rate levels are particularly unusual.

Information that does not amount to market abuse

Trading information

1.21   The unrestricted use of order-flow information does not amount to market abuse. This follows the proposals put forward in the first draft Code of Market Conduct ('the Code')[1] to the effect that information concerning a person's own, or any other person's, intention to deal (or not deal) in any qualifying investment product would not be caught by the provisions of the criminal résume. The exception to this is in respect of take-overs. This exemption should not be interpreted to suggest that the FSA is condoning or promoting front-running, and there will continue to be a conduct of business requirement to cover the use of order-flow information. Compliance officers will have to ensure that authorised firms are conducting relationships with customers in accordance with accepted and defined principles. This effectively means it will no longer be sufficient to argue that the behaviour was common market practice[2].

1 The Market Code may, among other things, specify:
    (a) descriptions of behaviour that, in the opinion of the FSA, amounts to market abuse;
    (b) descriptions of behaviour that, in the opinion of the FSA, does not amount to market abuse; and
    (c) factors that, in the opinion of the FSA, are to be taken into account in determining whether or not behaviour amounts to market abuse.
2 What is required is adherence to the Principles for Business No 5.

Take-over bid

1.22 It will not be market abuse if the person dealing is the offeror (or potential offeror, or someone acting for him) providing that he is acquiring an equity stake (in the target company) solely for the benefit of the offeror and for the sole purpose of pursuing the bid. It is therefore permissible that an offeror may deal in the target company shares to build a stake in the target company, but he may not undertake any other type of transaction in the target company's shares (or other investments). For example, it would amount to market abuse if the offeror was to attempt transactions in qualifying investments that demonstrated exposure risk to movements in the price of the target company's shares.

1.23 Details of what constitutes market abuse, with examples, will be contained in the Code. Under the FSMA 2000, the FSA is required to produce a code to give guidance to market participants. There have been two draft Codes produced so far, and in response to the comments made by industry a number of amendments have been made. Compliance personnel should not expect that when the final version is produced every conceivable eventuality will be covered. The Code is designed to provide clarity and certainty, but is not an exhaustive description of every type of misconduct that might be encountered.

1.24 The approach towards market abuse is consistent with the overall approach taken by the FSA; that is to be proactive in preventing all types of criminal behaviour. To this end, the compliance community can expect to see clear evidence of the FSA adopting a risk-based approach to regulation, with prevention through early misconduct identification being at the forefront of activity.

1.25 Under s 118 of the FSMA 2000 it is for the Treasury to decide to which markets these provisions apply. The vehicle for this is the Prescribed Markets and Qualifying Investments Order. A draft of this Order was produced in June 1999. The Treasury can also determine the range of investments that are to be considered as qualifying investments in relation to those markets. It is the intention of the Treasury that not only the trading of securities will be included, but also markets in commodity derivatives and financial futures.

Financial crimes and perimeter offences

1.26   The reduction of financial crime is one of the central aims of the FSMA 2000. The role of the FSA is to reduce the extent to which it is possible for business to be used as a conduit through which financial crime can be committed. Section 6 of the FSMA 2000 defines financial crime as any offence involving fraud, dishonesty or misconduct in or misuse of information relating to a financial market or handling the proceeds of crime.

1.27   It is seen from this that the FSA has the power to investigate a very wide range of criminal offences. However, the FSA will not exercise its powers without consultation and co-operation with other law enforcement agencies. The overall objective for the FSA is not to prosecute criminal offences but to raise the awareness of the business community to its inadvertent involvement in crime, in particular the laundering of the illicit proceeds of crime through regulated persons.

1.28   As a general principle, the FSA has taken a position that the laundering of money poses risks in relation to two other key objectives: market confidence and the protection of consumers. Whilst the FSMA 2000, s 6 also captures criminal conduct apart from money laundering, there is no further mention of other offences in the Act. The FSA has devoted very little commentary to any of the other offences, and the consultation documentation to date has not taken this further. On this basis it would be reasonable to proceed with the view that the FSA will not investigate offences of fraud or handling stolen goods under the Theft Act 1968[1], but that if those matters are brought to its attention it will liaise with the appropriate enforcement agency and co-operate with that body.

1   Section 15 and 15A offences of deception and s 22 offences of handling stolen goods contained in the Theft Act 1968. In cases of money laundering there is considerable overlap between the provisions of the Theft Act 1968 and the Criminal Justice Act 1993 (as inserted into the Criminal Justice Act 1988). Consequently, it is often the case that matters are proceeded against under the specific money laundering provisions in the Criminal Justice Act 1993 rather than under the Theft Act 1968. Evidentially it is also easier to prove the offences under the Criminal Justice Act 1993 than it is under the Theft Act 1968.

1.29   The roles of the enforcement agencies remain unchanged, and the FSA complements the existing arrangements. To this end, the FSA will concentrate on anti-money laundering and monitoring the activities of regulated persons to prevent its incidence.

Perimeter offences

1.30   In this section the term 'perimeter offences' is introduced. These offences are those which sit at the edge of the boundary between lawful and unlawful financial services conduct and are not captured within the mainstream offences of market abuse or financial crime. The offences discussed are all contained within the FSMA 2000 and are typically those offences that may be associated with other criminal offending within and outside of this Act.

1.31   There are ten perimeter offences that the FSA has the power to investigate. The policy on conducting investigations supports the view that in order to maintain public confidence it is necessary to use enforcement powers against authorised and unauthorised market participants. However, it should be noted that the criminal provisions are not restrictive, and the FSA has the discretion to seek civil redress if it is considered more appropriate in the particular circumstances. Significantly, and particularly in respect of financial promotion offences, when reading this section it should be remembered that there is no distinction between an advertisement and unsolicited calls[1]. The Treasury can adjust the scope of the FSMA 2000's financial promotion regime to accommodate national and international developments, and it can be expected that as the use of e-commerce develops there will be adjustments made.

1   Commonly referred to as 'cold calling', as per the Financial Services Act 1986.

1.32   Under the FSMA 2000, s 19 there is a general prohibition on unauthorised persons conducting regulated activities in the UK. This is referred to as the 'general prohibition', and contravention of this provision is a criminal offence. Furthermore, any agreement during the course of an activity in contravention of the prohibition may render the agreement unenforceable.

1.33   What is meant by 'carried on in the UK' is defined in the FSMA 2000, s 418; however it should be noted that these provisions apply to terrestrial transactions. Transactions conducted via the Internet are not subject to the same provisions, and regulation of these matters is still under development. It is unlikely that this will be resolved before N3 and certainly not before N2.

1.34   Under this part the discussion refers to a business that is 'carried on' in the UK and is in accordance with the EC directives on the matter. A person is carrying on a regulated activity in the UK in four circumstances:

- the head office or registered offices are in the UK but the financial business is conducted within another European Economic Area ('EEA') state;
- the head office or registered office is in the UK and they operate as managers of schemes, and other persons are invited to become participants in the scheme;
- the head office or registered office is in the UK, they conduct business outside the EEA but they direct day to day management of the activities from the UK; and
- they do not have a head office or registered offices in the UK, they do not deal with UK customers but they operate from an establishment maintained in the UK.

1.35 It is also an offence to falsely claim to be authorised when you are not[1] and to breach the financial promotions provisions contained in s 21 of the FSMA 2000. Both these offences attract custodial sentences and, in addition, the fine in respect of advertising is linked to the number of days that the material was on public display.

1   FSMA 2000, s 24.

1.36 Schedule 4 of the FSMA 2000 gives effect to the right that persons have to provide financial services that are established under other EEA states. These are rights that extend beyond those covered by Sch 3, the 'EEA Passport Rights'. What the rights under Sch 4 amount to is the ability of a person authorised in one member state to conduct financial services business in another state provided that the host state's provisions meet the minimum standards set by the EU. The definitions that are applied to terms such as 'EEA firm' or 'Treaty firm' are contained in s 31 of the FSMA 2000. Under the Schedule, notice must be given by the firm concerned to the effect that it proposes to exercise its right to conduct business in the UK. Failure to give proper notice is a criminal offence. It is also an offence to knowingly or recklessly provide false or misleading information.

Fit and proper persons

1.37 Under Part V of the FSMA 2000 the FSA has a wide range of powers available to it to ensure that individuals conducting financial services business are 'fit and proper' persons. It is recognised that there is considerable diversity in the range of activities conducted within the sector, and in response to this a number of the bodies within the industry have created in-house regulatory and disciplinary procedures. Under the FSMA 2000, s 56 the FSA may make orders that prohibit individuals who it considers are not 'fit and proper' from performing regulated activity functions. Prohibitions can be blanket and cover all activities or specific ones. The order may be varied or revoked.

Remedies

1.38 A person found to be in breach of a prohibition order, by performing or agreeing to perform a function, commits a criminal offence under the FSMA 2000, s 56. Additionally, a firm who engages a prohibited person is liable to disciplinary action. In circumstances such as these, where a firm (or other authorised person) has employed a person subject to an order then s 71 of the FSMA 2000 could be invoked by the firm's customer in the event of a loss being incurred.

1.39   Section 71 is the vehicle through which an action may be brought for damages if a person has suffered a loss as a result of an authorised person acting in breach of a duty imposed under s 56 of the FSMA 2000. It should be borne in mind that this provision also captures those participants who are exempt from the general prohibition, eg those who are a member of a professional body designated by the Treasury, and the regulated activity provided is incidental and complementary to the mainstream professional activity, such as legal services. In addition, the regulated activity must not relate to certain sensitive products such as life insurance. It is not possible to identify the entire range of 'sensitive products' as this has yet to be determined by the Treasury.

1.40   Part XI of the FSMA 2000 sets out the powers of the FSA to commence investigations, to demand the production of information and materials, and to enter premises to search for evidence. Any person who obstructs the FSA in the exercise of these powers commits a criminal offence.

1.41   The powers conferred under Part XI are in addition to any conferred elsewhere in the FSMA 2000, for example where the FSA has the power to demand information from unauthorised persons in connection with an application for authorisation or recognition. Under Part XI the FSA is entitled to require information on an ad hoc basis. The thinking behind this is that it will supplement the FSA's power to require authorised persons to supply information on a routine basis.

1.42   Under the FSMA 2000, s 177, if a person fails to comply with a requirement imposed under Part XI they are liable to be held in contempt. A person who knows or suspects that an investigation is being conducted will commit a criminal offence if he falsifies or conceals or destroys any document which he knows or suspects is relevant to an investigation. He also commits a criminal offence if he permits another to commit any of the above.

1.43   The wording of this provision is drafted sufficiently widely to ensure that if anyone suspected that an investigation was about to be started then any obstruction or interference with that course of action would amount to criminal conduct.

1.44   Nothing under Part XI affects the right that surrounds 'protected items' as described in s 413 of the FSMA 2000. This means that the FSA cannot demand the production or disclosure of items that are materially identical to items subject to professional privilege[1].

1   As defined under s 10 of the Police and Criminal Evidence Act 1984.

Authorisation

1.45   Part XII of the FSMA 2000 is concerned with control over authorised persons. Specifically, a person who proposes to increase the level of control or to actually acquire control over a UK authorised person must notify the FSA and obtain its permission. The FSA may approve such a move or it may object, or it may attach conditions to its approval. If a person is seeking to decrease (reduce) control over a UK authorised person then their liability is restricted to notifying the FSA – they do not need approval. Failure to comply with these requirements is a criminal offence under the FSMA 2000, s 191.

1.46   There are four offences under s 191:

- failure to comply with notification requirements. This applies to notification of increase or reduction in control;
- carrying out a proposal before the FSA has given approval. The time frame for this is three months beginning with the date when the FSA first received the notice, and the FSA has not responded by either giving approval or issuing a warning notice;
- in cases where the FSA has issued a warning notice it will be a further offence if he carries out a proposal before the FSA has decided whether to follow up the warning notice with a notice of objection; and
- acquiring control in contravention of an objection notice.

1.47   It is also an offence to fail to notify the FSA within 14 days of becoming aware of a duty to notify. This means that if a person proposes to increase or reduce control and is not aware of the need to notify, then as soon as he is aware of the need to notify he must do so. If, after 14 days from the day when he first became aware, he has not informed the FSA, this will also constitute a criminal offence.

1.48   The FSMA 2000 requires authorised persons to appoint an actuary or auditor if they are not already under an obligation elsewhere to do so, for example under Companies Act requirements. It follows that it will be a criminal offence to deliberately mislead a person so appointed. Section 346 of the FSMA 2000 applies to an authorised person as well as an officer, controller or manager of an authorised person, and the offence is complete if a person knowingly or recklessly gives an auditor or actuary information that is false or misleading.

1.49   The FSA will hold a public record of authorised persons. It has a responsibility to ensure that the information it has is accurate and reliable, and the nature of this process will inevitably mean that the FSA is also in possession of confidential information. It will also be in possession of potentially damaging information that may lead to an investigation and subsequent prosecution. It is therefore imperative that the information in the possession of the FSA remains confidential. It may transpire that the FSA will be required to share information with other domestic and international regulators and enforcement agencies. The disclosure of information through 'gateways' is already subject to domestic and EC constraints. It is the nature of financial services investigations that a number of bodies may hold information that may assist the FSA; typically this could be the Department of Trade and Industry, the Inland Revenue or the Director General of Fair Trading.

1.50   Under the FSMA 2000, s 352 it is an offence for any person to make an unauthorised disclosure of confidential information. Confidential information means[1] information that relates to the business or other affairs of any person that was received by the primary recipient for the purposes of the discharge of any functions for the FSA. Typically this will mean the information supplied to or gathered by investigators appointed under the FSMA 2000.

1   See the FSMA 2000, s 348(2)(a), (b), (c).

1.51   Material that is not confidential would include items that are in the public domain or are formed in such a way that the material is not attributable to any one individual.

1.52   Certain materials may be treated as information that may be disclosed dependent upon the circumstances; for example if proceedings are being brought for a criminal offence committed under the FSMA 2000 or the Criminal Justice Act 1993 ('CJA 1993') for insider dealing. Additionally, matters that are put before the FSA tribunal may be treated as information that is available to be disclosed and therefore will not be caught by the provisions of the FSMA 2000, s 352.

1.53   The last offence within this part is that of misleading the FSA. Under the FSMA 2000, s 398 it is an offence to knowingly or recklessly give false or misleading information to the FSA. This should be viewed as an offence separate from any other offences of this nature contained within the FSMA 2000, eg under s 177(4) where there is a requirement to supply information to investigators.

1.54   It is also an offence under s 399 of the FSMA 2000 to knowingly or recklessly mislead or give false information to the Director General of Fair Trading[1].

1   This puts into force the provisions of s 44 of the Competition Act 1998.

1.55   As we have seen previously in the legislation, the offences captured in s 400 are applicable to individuals, partners, directors and officers of bodies corporate (FSMA 2000, s 400).

Criminal offences contained in Acts other than the FSMA 2000

Money laundering

1.56   The role of the FSA in the prevention and detection of money laundering is described in Consultation Paper 46. It is not the intention of the FSA that it will prosecute offences of money laundering, but rather that the FSA will co-operate with existing criminal law enforcement agencies to add value, through the regulatory process, to stimulating good practice and preventing occurrences of money laundering. The authority to do this is contained in s 6 of the FSMA 2000 which details the legislature's expectation that the FSA will be proactive in preventing financial crime.

1.57   The law criminalising money laundering is not within the FSMA 2000; however the FSA does have the power under this Act to make rules. To this end, it may 'make rules in relation to the prevention and detection of money laundering in connection with the carrying on of regulated activities by authorised persons'. Section 146 of the FSMA 2000 and, as we have seen previously in this part, the FSA, may, under the FSMA 2000, s 400, institute proceedings (except in Scotland) for a range of criminal offences including money laundering.

'Money laundering' is defined in Consultation Paper 46 as follows[1]:

> 'Money laundering is the process by which the proceeds of crime are converted into assets which appear to have a legitimate origin, so that they can be retained permanently or recycled to fund further crime.'

1   Consultation Paper 46, p 7.

Legislation

1.58   Recognition of the offence has a respectable history, and since the early 1980s there have been a number of national and international initiatives; these include the Basle Committee statement in 1988, the UN Vienna Convention of 1988, the establishment of the Financial Action Task Force ('FATF') by the G7 group in 1989, a Council of Europe Convention in 1990 and an EC Directive in 1991. A second Directive is currently being prepared.

1.59   Nationally, money laundering is a criminal offence under the Drug Trafficking Offences Act 1986, the Criminal Justice Act 1988 ('CJA 1988'), the Prevention of Terrorism (Temporary Provisions) Act 1989, the Criminal Justice (International Co-operation) Act 1990, the Northern Ireland (Emergency Provisions) Act 1991 and the Criminal Justice Act 1991.

1.60   It is clear from the list in para **1.59** that there is a considerable volume of legislation already in place to curb the practice of converting illicit money into licit use. The FSMA 2000 should therefore be viewed as supportive legislation but not ancillary[1]:

> 'In the FSA's view, this complex legal background is not likely to be wholly abandoned or radically altered either internationally or within the UK. However it is unlikely to remain wholly static ... On a wider international front, the G8 and FATF are actively promoting continuing improvement in the laws and resources needed throughout the world to fight money laundering.'

It is against this complexity and potential change that the following discussion is set.

1   Consultation Paper 46, p 8.

1.61   When discussing the range of criminal offences for which the FSA may prosecute, it is important to bear in mind that the FSA is a regulator and therefore the focus of its activity will always be driven by implementing and supporting systems and controls that stimulate good practice. The FSA will not seek to duplicate the established roles performed by authorities such as the police, the Serious Fraud Office ('SFO') and the National Criminal Intelligence Service ('NCIS'). It will, however, convey information to these authorities under its remit to prevent financial crimes and it may bring additional criminal proceedings in respect of matters contained within the FSMA 2000.

Regulation

1.62   The money laundering rules written by the FSA are intended to have wide application. At present some professionals (such as solicitors) are regulated by Recognised Professional Bodies. These firms are treated as exempt from the need to be authorised under the FSMA 2000, and it follows that for this class of firm they will be exempt from the money laundering rules. In the case where a firm is regulated but also conducts 'exempt regulated activities' then the money laundering rules will apply, except in respect of the exempt regulated activities that they conduct.

This does not mean to say that the provisions of the legislation outside of the FSMA 2000 do not apply – they certainly do – and the Money Laundering Regulations 1993 (SI 1993/1933) will have full effect.

The Money Laundering Regulations 1993

1.63   These Regulations became effective on 1 April 1994. They apply to financial institutions (as defined in the Regulations) and place a responsibility on the defined institutions to implement administrative procedures to prevent money laundering. The Regulations are not to be confused with the CJA 1993, which also deals with money laundering. The CJA 1993 was passed in response to an EC Directive on money laundering (EC 91/308), and this Act seeks to harmonise all the laws relating to money laundering, including the laws relating to money laundering and terrorism, drug trafficking and any other relevant criminal conduct. The CJA 1993 applies to everyone – all UK persons and businesses. The Money Laundering Regulations 1993 are additional to the Act and only apply to firms who are operating in the UK financial sector. The main point of reference for all money laundering offences is the CJA 1988 as amended by the CJA 1993.

1.64   There are a number of important differences between the contents of the Money Laundering Regulations 1993 and the FSMA 2000, in particular the terminology employed to define the scope of 'business activity'. Regulation 4 of the 1993 Regulations defines the meaning of 'relevant business activity' and specifies nine categories of business activity that are captured:

- deposit-taking when authorised under the Banking Act 1987;
- building society deposits;
- National Savings Bank business;
- Credit Union business (as defined under the Credit Unions Act 1979 or the Credit Unions (Northern Ireland) Order 1985);
- activities regulated as 'home' activities by a European institution;
- investment business under the terms of the Financial Services Act 1986;
- raising loans by the Director of National Savings;
- a range of activities contained within the Annex to the Second Banking Co-ordination Directive. This will include activities such as accepting deposits and other repayable funds from the public, lending, financial leasing and offering the provision of financial services in futures and options and transferable securities; and
- insurance business activities covered by arts 6 or 27 of the First Life Directive.

1.65   The FSMA 2000 replicates a number of these categories, for example in respect of the activities of building societies and deposit taking by banks. However, there are exceptions: for example the activities of a bureau de change are subject to the Money Laundering Regulations 1993 but not to the FSMA 2000, and the scope of general insurance work is governed by the FSMA 2000 but is not captured by the 1993 Regulations. To this end, the FSA has choices that it can exercise: it can either apply or disapply the FSA Rules in respect of certain activities. At present it is the view of the FSA that it will disapply the rules in respect of general insurance business and work within the parameters of the Money Laundering Regulations 1993 on this matter. However, it should be noted that this position remains open to debate and the FSA has the option to change its position in the future[1].

1   See further Consultation Paper 46, p 9.

1.66   The combined effect of all the legislation is that it is[1]:

' ... an offence for any person (individual or corporation) to provide assistance to a criminal to obtain, retain, transfer, remit, conceal or invest funds. If that person knows or suspects that the funds are proceeds of criminal activity then it is an offence if it is not reported at the earliest opportunity. In some cases, ie terrorist funding or the offences of concealing or transferring, it will be an offence if the person should have suspected that the funds are the proceeds of criminal conduct.'

1   Money Laundering 1, Introduction, FSA, 30 June 1999, p 1. Available at
     http://www.fsa.gov.uk.

1.67   If a financial institution is aware that a party is seeking an order for discovery which might require the institution to disclose information that may be prejudicial to a criminal investigation then the institution must inform the NCIS as soon as possible. The NCIS will then be responsible for deciding how the application should be dealt with.

1.68   The NCIS may permit partial disclosure. If the applicant is not satisfied with this it must be explained to the applicant that the matter may need to be decided by the courts. The applicant may not be informed of the court's involvement, particularly where a high degree of confidentiality is sought by the NCIS.

1.69   It may also be the case that matters are not suitable to be resolved in open court. In circumstances such as these, where an applicant is not present in court, a transcript of the proceedings must be made and these are to be released to the applicant once the NCIS have agreed there is no longer a need for secrecy.

1.70   The onus of proof rests throughout with the NCIS. It is required to satisfy the court of the need for non-disclosure. In the unlikely circumstances where the NCIS did not co-operate with the financial institution responsible for seeking an order, then in the first instance the court could properly draw an inference that no prejudice would be likely to occur and therefore the court could rightly make a disclosure order without putting the institution at risk of prosecution by the complainant.

This final point effectively deals with the potential problem of a financial institution becoming a constructive trustee due to the suspicions that the institution had about the provenance of funds deposited by an account holder.

The money laundering offences

1.71   The list of offences that are captured by the remit of the FSA is not wholly inclusive as there are a few offences related to money laundering that are unlikely to involve those connected with the provision of financial services, and these offences are more appropriately caught by mainstream criminal offending; for example some, but not all, of the provisions relating to money laundering and drugs trafficking.

1.72   The FSA have produced a Money Laundering Sourcebook that is designed to provide guidance on arrangements for effective systems and controls to prevent the financial sector becoming a conduit through which illicit funds are transferred and 'cleaned'. However, this Sourcebook relates only to regulatory requirements and not to the criminal law. Consequently, the Sourcebook is not relevant for supervisory guidance for the purposes of reg 5(3) of the Money Laundering Regulations 1993.

1.73   Regulation 5(3) of the Money Laundering Regulations 1993 stipulates that:

> 'In determining whether a person has complied with any of the requirements of paragraph (1) above [No person shall carry on relevant financial business unless they have adopted procedures to identify and prevent money laundering] a court may take account of (a) any relevant supervisory or regulatory guidance which applies to that person, (b) in a case where no guidance falling within sub-paragraph (a) applies, any other relevant guidance issued by a body that regulates, or is representative of, any trade, profession, business or employment carried on by that person.'

1.74   The FSA does not propose to take on the prosecution of money laundering offences contained within the CJA 1993 or the Money Laundering Regulations 1993, but it does have a statutory duty to report to the NCIS any suspicions it has in respect of money laundering activities by financial service providers. The over-arching role of the FSA is responsibility to ensure compliance with the 1993 Regulations.

1.75   For the purposes of money laundering and the involvement of the FSA, the following offences apply:

- Providing assistance

    The offences are captured under s 93A (assisting another to retain the benefit of criminal conduct), s 93B (acquisition, possession or use of proceeds of criminal conduct), or s 93C (concealing or transferring the proceeds of criminal conduct) of the CJA 1988 (as amended).

- Tipping off

  The FSA-issued Money Laundering Sourcebook advises financial service providers that prejudicing an investigation by 'tipping off' a suspect, or third party (an offence under s 93D of the CJA 1988) will be an offence that the FSA has the power to investigate and prosecute. However, under the schedule of offences provided at Annex A, p 25 of Consultation Paper 46 the tipping off offence is not listed. It would be safe to assume that this is an oversight as the offence will be one that is within the remit of offences that the FSA can investigate and prosecute.

- Assisting another with or being the principal in concealing or transferring the proceeds of drug trafficking is an offence that the FSA has the power to investigate and prosecute (Drug Trafficking Act 1994, s 49), as are the related offences of assisting another person to retain the benefit of drug trafficking (s 50) and acquiring, possessing or using the proceeds of drug trafficking, terrorism, or other relevant conduct (s 51).

1.76   There are two points to make in connection with the money laundering offences that relate to drugs and terrorism. For the person operating in the financial sector the knowledge or suspicion that is acquired is that which is obtained during the course of his employment. Second, although the schedule does not make mention of the further related offence – failing to disclose knowledge of suspicion of money laundering offences (under the Drug Trafficking Act 1994) – this is clearly captured by the contents of the Sourcebook at 3.1 under the main obligations imposed.

1.77   There are six further money laundering-related offences outlined in the schedule. One of these deals with concealment under international co-operation obligations, and the remainder are specific to jurisdiction issues in Northern Ireland and Scotland.

1.78   It is the intention of the FSA that the relationship between the FSA rules and the Money Laundering Regulations 1993 will be that they are similar but separate from each other. It would appear that the FSA is seeking to strike a balance between effective prevention and a workable, rather than overly burdensome and restrictive, set of rules, notwithstanding the caveat that the FSA has the statutory power to amend the Rules if and when necessary.

1.79   There is a general requirement on firms to maintain and keep records. This is contained within the general rule (X16 in Consultation Paper 35). There is a difference, however, in respect of the requirement to retain records that relate to financial promotions (under the general rule records must be kept for three years) and a requirement to retain records under the money laundering provisions. In respect of the latter, records must be kept for five years.

1.80   The applicable periods are:

- in relation to identification evidence that appertains to a customer, the five-year period runs from the period when the relationship between the firm and the customer ended;
- in respect of a transaction between the firm and customer during the five-year period, records must be retained for five years from the date when the transaction was concluded;
- if the matter relates to insolvency then the five-year period commences from the date of the insolvency; and
- in all other cases it is five years from when the information was obtained or the initial record was created.

1.81   As a general principle, the rules relating to money laundering apply to all market participants. However, there are parts of the Money Laundering Sourcebook that only apply to firms and not sole traders. Typically these are areas such as the need to appoint a Money Laundering Regulation Officer ('MLRO'). Sole traders, that is individuals who are authorised persons, with no employees apart from themselves, are advised to refer to Annex A, Consultation Paper 46, p 18 for the relevant list.

Insider dealing

1.82   The introduction of the FSMA 2000 means that all market participants will now be subject to one civil regime for the control of market abuse. As commented on previously, this provision has not been without its critics and a considerable body of opinion believes that the new offences contained within market abuse are in fact criminal, and in many respects duplicitous of existing criminal provisions under Part V of the CJA 1993. This is not the view of the FSA, and accordingly there are offences contained within the FSMA 2000 that the government maintains are civil, and criminal offences outside of the FSMA 2000 within the CJA 1993.

1.83   It is the view of the government that the core of efficient regulation is the prevention of insider dealing. As a criminal offence insider dealing has been legislated against for the past 20 years, initially under Part V of the Companies Act 1980, but the opportunity to seek civil redress has been largely limited to an action being brought by the forerunner to the FSA, the Securities Investment Board, or the Treasury, under the Financial Services Act 1986, s 61. As regards the private investor, if they were able to overcome the hurdle of establishing loss as a result of a breach of Self Regulating Organisation ('SRO') rules, then they could seek redress under s 62 of the Financial Services Act 1986. However, the provisions of Part V of the CJA 1993 do not, of themselves, have any implications under civil law, and no contract can be deemed void or unenforceable by reason only that it constitutes an offence of insider dealing under s 52 of the CJA 1993.

1.84 One can see why there has been strong government support for the introduction of provisions under the FSA that allow victim redress at civil law as this completes the circle in respect of entire coverage of insider dealing as an offence at every level. Nevertheless the offences contained within the CJA 1993 do not have multiple application and they are limited in scope to individuals as principal offenders. Companies and artificial legal persons cannot be charged with the substantive criminal offence of insider dealing.

1.85 In respect of both the civil market abuse and criminal insider dealing and market manipulation offences, the FSA has the statutory authority to investigate and bring a prosecution. The power to institute criminal proceedings is contained within s 402 of the FSMA 2000. As for money laundering, the FSA has decided it will not bring prosecutions under the Money Laundering Regulations 1993. It will do so for transgressions under the FSMA 2000. This is not the case in respect of insider dealing, where the FSA has indicated that it may bring criminal prosecutions under the FSMA 2000 or the CJA 1993, but will not impose a sanction under the civil limb when a market participant has been prosecuted or finally acquitted in criminal proceedings if they have arisen out of the same facts. This part of the chapter will deal with the latter categories of offending: insider dealing and market abuse.

Part V of the CJA 1993

1.86 Part V introduced reforms required under Council Directive 89/592/EEC, and it replaced the Companies Securities (Insider Dealing) Act 1985. The CJA 1993 is broader in application than the former legislation and captures, for example, gilts and securities issued by public sector bodies and the extension of liability to professional intermediaries operating in off-market dealings; and the definition of securities is extended to include new instruments.

1.87 There is one main offence in the CJA 1993, s 52 which covers a range of criminal offending. This can be broken down into three areas: encouraging, dealing and disclosing in contravention of the provisions. The characteristics of the offence are that the information used or disclosed must be unpublished, of a specific nature and price sensitive. This means that there is considerably less generality under this Act than sections of the FSMA 2000. The information must be in relation to particular securities and not securities in general, the information must not be in the public domain, and if it were made public then it would be likely to have a significant effect on the price of any securities.

1.88 Undisclosed information is very similar in meaning to the term contained within the FSMA 2000. Under the CJA 1993 there are four circumstances when information is public:

- when it is published in accordance with the rules of a regulated market;
- when it is placed in records that are open to inspection by members of the public;
- when it can be readily obtained by those that are likely to deal in any of the securities to which the information relates; and
- when it is from a source that is already available to the public.

These categories are not exclusive, and the spirit of the provisions also incorporates public information to mean events such as viewing a disaster, which would clearly be available for any member of the public to witness, or materials where the public could have access to the information if it chose to do so, eg where a fee is payable for the information.

1.89   Essential information about the application of the CJA 1993, defences and penalties are contained within the 12 sections that follow the offence. Clarity of terms is not always apparent; for example inside information (s 57) is information that only an insider has. This should be interpreted to mean that a person has inside information and he knows that it is from an inside source. This suggests that the test is subjective and will depend on the view held by the person in possession of the information as to its 'insideness'. In terms of prosecuting the offence, this subjectivity means that the prosecution will have to prove to the criminal standard, beyond all reasonable doubt, that the defendant was aware that the information in his possession was from an inside source and was not 'public information' as defined in s 56 of the CJA 1993.

1.90   The provisions of the CJA 1993 have extensive territoriality. The offending conduct must take place on the UK markets or through an intermediary based in the UK. This means that not only will the offence be complete in the case where the markets used are UK markets, but that also in circumstances where the only link with the UK is the professional intermediary based here, albeit the deals are executed off-market it will still be an offence of insider dealing under the CJA 1993.

1.91   The drafting of the FSMA 2000 in respect of overlap with the CJA 1993 suggests that there are clearly two streams of offending: market abuse under the FSMA 2000 and insider dealing and market manipulation under the CJA 1993. Section 130(1)(b) of the FSMA 2000 informs market participants that the Treasury may issue written guidance for the purposes of helping the FSA determine the appropriate course of action where offences of market abuse or insider dealing are apparent.

1.92   Where there is evidence of an offence of making false claims that a person is authorised, contrary to the FSMA 2000, s 24, or where there is evidence of misleading investors, a s 397 offence, or where market abuse has been committed or insider dealing under the CJA 1993, the FSA may appoint inspectors to investigate[1].

1   FSMA 2000, s 168(2)(a).

1.93   The FSA may intervene in respect of a firm incoming to the UK at the request of, or for the purpose of assisting, the host state regulator[1]. The reference here to the CJA 1993 is explanatory, and it ensures that the functions of the host state regulator correspond with those exercised by the FSA in a number of ways, including in the prevention of insider dealing as defined under the CJA 1988.

1   FSMA 2000, s 195(3)(d).

1.94   Information held by authorities other than the FSA may be relevant for the purposes of an FSA investigation. To this end, the Inland Revenue is exempt from an obligation to maintain secrecy and is required to disclose relevant information to the FSA if an FSA-appointed investigator is conducting an investigation into a range of offences. The range of offences captured includes any criminal proceedings brought under the FSMA 2000 and also offences of insider dealing under the CJA 1993[1].

1   FSMA 2000, s 350(4)(c).

1.95   When the CJA 1993 was introduced there was a considerable volume of concern expressed about the draconian nature of the provisions[1]:

'Until the CJA [1993] has been in force for long enough to allow the city to become accustomed to its provisions there may still be some anxiety over reforms. However, the Act represents a far greater change in form than in substance. To the extent that initial reactions to the Bill were little short of hysterical, it could be said that the new law's bark was worse than its bite.'

Perhaps in due course the same will be said of the FSMA 2000.

1   White, M 'Insider Dealing and the Criminal Justice Act 1993', p 74 in Rider, B and Ashe, M (eds) *The Fiduciary, the Insider and the Conflict* (1995).

A comment on e-regulation

1.96   Some parts of the FSMA 2000 are not due to come into force until N2, July 2001, but in reality this date may well slip. In addition there are likely to be further amendments to the Act, and it is perhaps difficult to expect the FSA to say anything definitive as much is still under discussion; this position is reflected in the Consultation Papers. It is hoped that by N3 there will be evidence of a more integrated approach to regulation than has been the case over the past 20 years; in particular market users can legitimately expect that matters dealing with Internet regulation will be comprehensive but also straightforward and will promote the government's view that the UK should become a global centre for e-commerce.

1.97   Compliance with any EU Directives will continue to be crucial, particularly in respect of e-regulation. Future regulatory developments will need constantly checking against human rights developments and case law as it develops in the traditional 'wet signature' environment. It is the view of the FSA that for effective regulation intrusive powers are often needed. In view of this it is most likely that the development of criminal sanctions to curb e-crimes under the FSMA 2000 are likely to receive as many challenges as have been seen so far in respect of traditional criminal offending under the Act. In respect of financial coms, the current US model of regulation is attractive to the FSA and may represent the likely model for the future in the UK.

1.98   Transparency Directives are crucial. These are where the EU may ask a state to 'hold' or wait implementation until a EU Directive is in place. The FSA is currently waiting for the Department of Trade and Industry's interpretation of the EU Directive on e-commerce and a number of issues remain unresolved; for example the 'centre of activity' question (eg, where is the centre of activity for a company in respect of e-companies?). At present the door is open to dot.coms to forum shop to locate the jurisdiction where the regulatory rules are lax. This is likely to mean that the FSA will cover e-commerce regulation as 'guidance' only at this time rather than write specific rules. At present, what is a regulated e-activity is a matter of speculation; perhaps the best working model to date is that outlined in *Re Great Western Assurance*[1].

1   [1999] Lloyd's Rep IR 377, CA.

1.99   Given the developmental stage of e-regulation at this time, the area is not covered under this chapter. The FSA itself does not yet have sufficient information to decide on the best way forward in this area, but given the tenet of dual approach, civil and criminal sanctions that are applicable to those who commit offences in the real environment, it is most probable that the same model will be utilised for implementing sanctions against offending market participants in the virtual environment[1].

1   For a further discussion on these matters see Rutledge, G and Haines, J *Butterworths Compliance Series: Electronic Trading* (2001).

CHAPTER 2

Powers of investigation and challenges to the decision-making of the Financial Services Authority

Introduction

2.1

'The main focus of comment on the draft Bill has been on the disciplinary process. There has been a perception that the FSA internal procedures may lack fairness and transparency, or be unduly costly and burdensome, and that the FSA will be able to act as "prosecutor, judge and jury"1.'

1 House of Commons Joint Committee, First Report, VI: Discipline and Enforcement, Introduction, p 1.

2.2 The Financial Services Authority ('FSA') is currently producing an Enforcement Manual and guide to terms and definitions. Consultation Papers 65 and 65a are informed by earlier discussion documents Consultation Paper 17 ('Enforcing the new regime') and Consultation Paper 25 ('Enforcing the new perimeter'). It has now become FSA practice to invite responses to its publications, and as a result of this feedback substantial changes have been made to the most recent Papers. These changes include:

- the establishment of the Regulatory Decisions Committee, which will now become a committee of the FSA board and will become involved in some authorisation, supervision and regulatory enforcement cases. The emphasis is on ensuring that there not only appears to be a division of supervisory roles but that the separation is actual and, accordingly, there is no potential conflict of interests;
- proposals for a mediation scheme in cases where settlement discussions break down;
- statements of policy on financial penalties in cases of disciplinary breaches and matters of market abuse;
- proposals on the use of its power to cancel permission and take action against EEA firms; and

- the use of enforcement powers in respect of collective investment schemes, disqualification of auditors and actuaries and disapplication orders against members of the professions.

2.3   The current discussion documents are likely to result in working policy by N2. In the meantime the FSA have not resisted taking disciplinary action when warranted, as can be seen by the 159 cases of suspected regulatory contraventions investigated by the FSA in 1999/2000. It may well be argued by government and the FSA that the inclusion of the points outlined in para **2.2** will be sufficient to ensure that there is a clear separation of powers between investigation and enforcement. The compliance community may disagree. Perhaps this will only become clear over time as the disciplinary and prosecutorial powers are tested.

2.4   Some of the potentially intriguing problems that the earlier draft Consultation Papers raised have now been clarified. Firms will be notified when a matter is passed from suspension to enforcement, other than in exceptional circumstances where the investigation would be prejudiced by the disclosure. Also, when a firm is the subject of disciplinary action, FSA supervision staff will continue to have responsibility for the handling of all other regulatory matters within the firm.

2.5   The Financial Services and Markets Tribunal will be a first instance tribunal; it is the Enforcement Committee who will determine whether there is a case to answer. Throughout this process the firm or individual has the right to make written and oral submissions and take part in early settlement negotiations. If these break down then the next stage is to seek independent mediation. None of the RDC, except the chair, will be FSA staff, and the Enforcement Committee will operate independently of the FSA. It is anticipated by the FSA that enforcement action will be triggered by a breach of rules and not on the basis of a contravention of the Principles alone.

2.6   The independence of the Tribunal is guaranteed as it is part of the Court Service and not the FSA. Its function is to provide the opportunity for challenge and review to the decisions of the FSA, and the Tribunal has legislative authority to substitute its own conclusions for those of the FSA. It is proposed that appeals against decisions of the Tribunal will be to the Court of Appeal rather than to the High Court which, in effect, will hasten the appeals procedure considerably. It should be noted that appeal to the Tribunal is restricted to regulatory matters; there is no right of appeal to the Tribunal against the use of enforcement powers by the FSA when conducting a criminal investigation. Redress in this respect must be sought through judicial review.

Powers and enforcement procedures

2.7   Investigation and information gathering powers are contained in Parts X and XI of the Financial Services and Markets Act 2000 ('FSMA 2000'). The basis for these wide ranging provisions is that, in the opinion of the government, the new authority for the new millennium needs to have flexibility and strength to deal proportionately with a range of regulatory and criminal offences. A balance must be struck, however, between draconianism and intrusiveness on the one hand and efficiency and appropriate regulation in the interests of consumers on the other. The FSMA 2000 vests the following powers in the FSA:

- to require information and documents from authorised persons;
- to obtain a warrant and enter premises to search for and seize materials related to an investigation;
- to appoint investigators to conduct inquiries into persons and firms;
- to appoint investigators to conduct criminal investigations into authorised and unauthorised persons;
- to compel information from third parties where it is believed that he may have information relevant to a criminal investigation;
- to appoint investigators to conduct inquiries into collective investment schemes;
- to require an authorised person to commission a specialist report; and
- to conduct an investigation on behalf of an overseas regulator.

What follows is a detailed discussion of the specific powers referred to above with references made to the applicable sections and Parts of the FSMA 2000. This chapter concludes with a discussion of the rights that exist to challenge the decisions made by the FSA in respect of sanctions and criminal prosecutions.

2.8   Part X of the FSMA 2000 is the Rules and Guidance section. Section 138 is the first section in this Part, and it grants the FSA power to make rules that apply to authorised persons with regard to their carrying on of regulated and unregulated activities. These rules are referred to as 'general rules' and are specifically for the purpose of protecting the interests of consumers. There is no other basis for the FSA making rules under this part; however, there need not be a direct relationship between the persons affected by the rules and those parties that it seeks to protect. The example cited in the explanatory notes is that rules can be made to protect the interests of beneficiaries of trusts.

2.9   The scope of this Part is theoretically global, as territoriality is not limited. However, in application it is likely to be broad in respect of UK-based activities, but perhaps limited when applied to those exercising passport rights in the UK. This is largely due to the fact that general rules are unlikely to attempt to restrict the activities which are currently regulated by the home state under the Single Markets Directive. Domestically the rules

27

will capture unregulated activities by regulating the systems and controls in place within a firm. The FSA in particular will need convincing that the conduct of business and advice given to customers is appropriate and that the capital reserves of the firm are sufficient.

Principles and rules

2.10 At this point a distinction is made between certain types of rules. They fall into two categories: rules with high levels of applicability and generality are called 'principles'. Principles are broad in coverage and are designed to set out the general standards of conduct expected by the FSA from those persons engaged in the supply of financial services. The use of the term 'principles' is rather confusing as it is used under the heading of 'rules' and can be created, as rules can also be, by the FSA. Principles with the meaning given here are separate from, and not to be confused with, statements of principle for approved persons under Part V of the FSMA 2000.

2.11 Detailed provisions that apply to specific areas of activity are 'rules'. Contravention of a rule will normally be sufficient to capture enforcement action by the FSA and liability for a private action for damages. The legislation has been drafted very widely at this point as, under the FSMA 2000, s 156, the FSA has power to make different rules for different market participants and in different and individual cases. This has clear implications in respect of the reasonableness issue that may be challenged as it would be hard to successfully argue that the FSA was unreasonable when equity in operation of the rules will not be a relevant issue for review. Perhaps the most useful indicator at this point is to remind compliance personnel that 'R' in the Handbook signifies a binding rule.

Provisions and guidance

2.12 Under s 149 of the FSMA 2000 the FSA may make rules that, if broken, will not lead to any disciplinary action. Any rule made under this part must clearly indicate its effect and also that the fact that there has been a breach of a rule under s 149 may be evidence of other breaches which may give rise to sanctions. It is for this reason that these provisions are referred to as 'evidential provisions' as they can be relied on as an indication of another breach. Evidential provisions are marked with an 'E' in the margin of the Handbook.

2.13 Under the FSMA 2000, s 157 the FSA will publish guidance on a number of matters, including its own rules and criminal offences captured under the FSMA 2000. Guidance notes will be marked 'G' in the handbook. To what extent guidance notes can be relied upon as evidence of attempted compliance with a rule or principle is unclear, and there is no commentary on this in the FSMA 2000. There is the possibility of a limited defence under legitimate expectation and taking all reasonable precautions; both of these will be discussed in greater detail in Chapter 3.

2.14   What the above amounts to is the FSA having legislative authority to create binding rules that have the force of law, but which have not been subjected to parliamentary scrutiny. Given that the FSA is a private company and not an arm of the legislature or executive, this is an unusual provision under English law as one normally expects to see secondary legislation, typically created by government departments, to be subject to parliamentary consensus. The view of the government is that the requirement to act reasonably, which is subject to judicial review, is itself sufficient safeguard.

2.15   Breach of a rule by an authorised person may result in public censure and fines, the issuing of injunctions and restitution. Details of the disciplinary measures are found in Parts XIV and XXV of the FSMA 2000 respectively.

For information regarding the procedural requirements that the FSA must satisfy when making rules, reference should be made to ss 152–155 of the FSMA 2000.

Requests for information and documents

2.16   The FSA may require a present or former authorised person to provide, by written notice, information or documents. This request cannot be a fishing trip, and the written notice must specify what information or documents are sought. The FSA is empowered to specify the place and date for delivery of the documents or information. Any person, natural or legal, who is:

- an authorised person;
- a formerly authorised person;
- a person connected with an authorised person (this is spelt out in sub-s (11) of s 165 of the FSMA 2000. It effectively captures partners or others who have at any time been part of a group of which an authorised person is a member);
- an operator, trustee or depository of an open-ended investment company;
- a recognised investment exchange; or
- a recognised clearing house

may be requested to supply information or documents. Requests may be by mail or in person through an appointed FSA investigator. It is of note that, although there is a general requirement on the FSA to act reasonably, the FSMA 2000 specifies that a demand for documents can be that they are supplied immediately. The information supplied must be in the form specified by the FSA.

2.17 The only limitations to the requirements in para **2.16** are that they 'may be imposed only so far as the investigator concerned reasonably considers the question, provision of information or the production of the document to be relevant to the purposes of the investigation'[1].

1 FSMA 2000, s 171.

Entry to premises and seizure of materials

2.18 Under the draft Bill it was intended that entry to premises would be without warrant. This was strongly contested, and the FSMA 2000, s 176 provides that entry is restricted to constables in possession of a warrant issued by a magistrate. A warrant will be granted if any one of the following three criteria apply:

- a person who has been requested to supply documents or information has failed to do so and on the premises are relevant documents or information; or
- the premises are the business premises of an authorised person or appointed representative, and a request for information or documents has not been complied with or the information or documents have been tampered with or destroyed; or
- there are grounds to believe a specific s 168 or s 284 offence has been or is being committed, and there is information or documents relevant to the investigation at those premises which could be required by the FSA but would not be produced, or might be removed, tampered with or destroyed.

2.19 If an authorised person is engaged in a serious offence and deliberately concealing or removing materials then the power of the FSA would be severely limited if entry by warrant could not be forced. A search warrant will authorise a constable to enter premises, by force if necessary, to search, seize, or take copies of, or extracts from, any documents or information, and require any person on the premises to provide an explanation of any such document or information or to state where it may be located. For the purposes of clarity the FSA will attempt to ensure that the appointed investigator's name appears on the warrant.

Information gathering and investigations

2.20 The FSMA 2000 specifically requires the FSA to describe its policies and procedures for exercising the enforcement powers when considering:

- imposing financial penalties on a firm or approved individuals;
- imposing fines for market abuse;
- conducting interviews on behalf of overseas regulators; and

- issuing a warning notice, decision notice or supervisory notice issued by the Regulatory Decisions Committee.

2.21   Part XI of the FSMA 2000 and Chapter 2 of the Enforcement Manual describe the formal powers that the FSA has to gather information and investigate. The first of these five discrete powers is that to require information and documents from authorised persons (FSMA 2000, s 165). This power is analogous with the powers contained in the predecessor legislation under the Financial Services Act 1986, s 104.

'167' investigations

2.22   People appointed to conduct a general investigation may be employees of the FSA or others engaged specifically for the investigation. A general investigation, defined under s 167 of the FSMA 2000, may be instigated by the FSA or the Secretary of State. The reason for initiating an investigation would be that there is good reason to believe that an authorised person or their appointed representative has committed an offence under the FSMA 2000.

2.23   If the investigator decides to exercise his authority to demand information or documents from those people who were formerly a member of the authorised person's group then he must notify these connected companies, partners or individuals, in writing, of his intentions.

2.24   The power to initiate an investigation is not limited to the activities of regulated business as under the FSMA 2000, s 167(5) business is defined as 'any part of a business even if it does not consist of carrying on regulated activities'.

2.25   The policy of exercising the FSA's investigatory powers is contained within 2.6–2.11 of Consultation Paper 65a. It is clear that the FSA takes cognisance of the broad range of powers within the FSMA 2000 and the use of powers is unlikely to be restricted to regulatory matters only and will most likely capture any of the activities of market participants, including supervisory guidance and the education of consumers. The powers will be used for the 'routine supervision' of firms or persons within a firm. The overall tenet of the use of powers under general provisions is that the FSA will instigate an investigation on a subjective basis dependent upon, in its view, the nature and seriousness of the conduct and also the attitude that the firm takes towards the FSA's involvement. Presumably the more accommodating a firm appears to be, the less likely the FSA is to feel that all of its powers need to be exercised.

2.26   As a guide to the type of activity likely to attract further FSA attention, a non-exhaustive list has been supplied in Consultation Paper 65a.

Six categories are listed, and they include conduct such as behaviour by a firm that is likely to prejudice the interests of consumers. This is no great surprise given that one of the pillars of the legislation is an increase in the level of protection afforded to financial services consumers.

2.27 As we have seen in para **2.15** a breach of rules, failing to meet threshold conditions on being a fit and proper person or committing a criminal offence under the FSMA 2000 will all be caught. The FSA will also concern itself with the ownership of firms and particularly where a person is believed to have a degree of influence over a firm.

2.28 Finally in this category are those acts that are of such severity that they are likely to cause serious public concern over the way in which a firm conducts its activities. Again, this is a subjective view, but it would clearly be influenced by physical evidence from members of the public.

Specific investigations

2.29 Apart from general investigations there is also the power to conduct specific investigations, or '168' investigations as they will no doubt be referred to in due course. As seen in para **2.25**, an investigation may be into a regulatory or criminal offence, but the difference between '167' and '168' investigations lies in the powers of the investigator. In this instance they are greater than those permitted when conducting a general investigation. The FSMA 2000 refers to '168' investigations as 'Particular Investigations'; this means that the FSA may appoint investigators where it appears that some specific contravention or offence may have been committed. These can be broken down into matters of a regulatory nature and those of a criminal nature.

2.30 Matters of a regulatory nature will include, for example:

- publishing details of a warning notice or decision (s 21 offence);
- acting without authorisation (s 23 offence);
- falsely claiming to be authorised or exempt (s 24 offence);
- failing to adhere to restrictions in respect of financial promotions (s 25 offence);
- failing to take reasonable care under s 56 prohibition orders;
- failing to ensure that a controlled function is not performed by an unauthorised person (s 59(1), (2) offence);
- provisions made prohibiting a European Economic Area ('EEA') firm from carrying on (s 138(6A) offence);
- a breach of insurance business regulations under s 142;
- not being a fit and proper person;
- acting in breach of a principle; and
- breaching an FSA rule.

2.31   Breaches of the insurance regulations applies to offences under ss 21 and 238 of the FSMA 2000. The offence commonly known as 'cold-calling' under the Financial Services Act 1986 is dealt with under s 21 of the FSMA 2000. Inducements to participate in a collective investment scheme are offences under the FSMA 2000, s 238. Collective investment schemes are subject to considerable discussion under the FSMA 2000, but in general they are largely a replication of the provisions contained in the previous Financial Services Act 1986. Investigators may be appointed to inquire into the affairs of the manager or trustee of any unit trust scheme, as well as the affairs of the operator, trustee or depository of any such unit trust or collective investment scheme operating in the UK. The affairs of investment companies with variable capital ('ICVCs') are not dealt with under this section. However, it is anticipated that the Treasury will give the FSA powers to appoint investigators and make inquiries into directors and depositories of ICVCs.

2.32   The changes under the FSMA 2000 are regarding authorised unit trust investments and borrowing powers. The FSMA 2000 also permits the Treasury to create regulations in connection with the creation and operation of open-ended investment companies. The FSA will deal with this entire area as 'rules'. Relevant definitions are specified in the FSMA 2000, s 235, and these are a replication of the familiar terminology employed under the Financial Services Act 1986, s 75.

2.33   During the legislative process through parliament there was considerable pressure put on the government to restrict the territoriality of the FSMA 2000. The government resisted and we see no territorial limits to the application of the above powers. In theory, the FSA may apply the sanctions to any authorised person other than a passporting EEA firm. This means that the activities of an overseas person, who conducts business from an overseas location, are within the scope of the FSA's rules and sanctions.

2.34   Before reviewing the application of the powers relating to criminal offending it is worth considering a range of miscellaneous ancillary matters that supplement the general rule-making power. Under the FSMA 2000, s 139 the FSA can make rules in respect of the handling of client money by authorised persons. This provision may take precedence over established principles, for example by requiring that a statutory trust is created to protect client money from creditors in the event of an authorised person's insolvency. This section also allows the FSA to make rules that require a 'cooling off' period after a customer has entered into an agreement. These unilateral provisions will formalise investor protection along lines similar to those already established, for example under the Insurance Companies Act 1982 where persons entering into long-term insurance contracts have 14 days during which time they can cancel the policy and recover the premium paid.

2.35 Section 139 of the FSMA 2000 also reiterates established case law where the courts have clarified the status of banks as constructive trustees in circumstances where money has been wrongfully withdrawn from client accounts. Under s 139 a bank will be liable where it is established that the bank had knowledge that the withdrawal was wrong and it had deliberately failed to make relevant enquiries. The test of deliberately failing to make enquiries will be objective and is based on the notion that the bank will have failed to discharge its duty if it fails to make enquiries that 'a reasonable and honest person would have done' (s 139(2)(b)). The FSA proposes to make comprehensive client money rules, and further reference should be made to The Conduct of Business Sourcebook, Consultation Paper 45a.

2.36 Specific investigations of a criminal nature are:

- any perimeter offence: failure to comply with a requirement to assist an investigator (s 177 offence); failing to notify the authority of a change of circumstances in respect of acquisition, or of a change in the control of a firm or control over an authorised person (s 191 offence); giving false or misleading information to an appointed actuary or auditor (s 346 offence); giving false or misleading statements (s 397 offence); making false or misleading statements to an investigator (s 398 offence); a contravention of EEA state provisions (Sch 4);
- market manipulation (s 341);
- insider dealing (encouraging or disclosing) under Part V of the Criminal Justice Act 1993;
- market abuse; and
- money laundering.

2.37 There is no mention of the power to investigate any financial crime as defined in the FSMA 2000, s 6; and whereas misconduct is captured, handling stolen goods and fraud or dishonesty are not mentioned in Consultation Paper 65a. Whether this is an oversight or intentional is unclear.

2.38 Appointed investigators have varying degrees of power dependent upon the type of investigation they are appointed to conduct. If appointed under the FSMA 2000, s 168(1) and (4) the powers are different from those appointed under the FSMA 200, s 168(2).

Section 168(1) and (4) investigations

2.39 A person appointed under this section has the same powers as an investigator under the general provisions (FSMA 2000, s 167) and, in addition, specific powers. These specific powers are further divided under the FSMA 2000 into types of investigation: either s 168(1) and (4) or s 168(2). Section 168(1) applies:

- where investigations are being conducted into a contravention of insurance business regulations (s 142);
- where any perimeter offence has been committed and a person falsifies, conceals, destroys or disposes of information relevant to the investigation (s 177);
- where the appointed person fails to notify changes in the controlling interests of an authorised firm (s 191);
- where the appointed person provides misleading information to an auditor or actuary (s 346);
- where the appointed person provides misleading information to the FSA (s 398); and
- with Sch 4 Treaty rights;

and s 168 (4):

- where a person acts without permission (s 20);
- in cases of money laundering;
- due to contravention of a rule;
- where a person is not a fit and proper person;
- where a person acts in contravention of a prohibition order;
- where a person fails to comply with s 56(6), ie to prevent a prohibited person from acting;
- where a person fails to gain appropriate FSA approval (s 59(1)); and
- where a person fails to comply with a principle.

2.40   It can be seen that the powers are not divided between regulatory and criminal offences and overall they appear arbitrary. The FSA may appoint an investigator under sub-s (2) of s 168 in cases of suspected insider dealing, a breach of a general prohibition, contraventions of the inducement provisions (ss 21 and 238) and in cases of market abuse. Quite why a distinction should be drawn between the powers to investigate one class of offence contained outside of the FSMA 2000, insider dealing, and another, money laundering, is and remains unclear.

2.41   Under the FSMA 2000, s 168(1) and (4) the investigator has the power to require a person, who is not the subject of the investigation, nor connected to the person subject to the investigation, to attend before him at a specified time and place and answer questions, or otherwise provide information as he may require, for the purposes of the investigation.

2.42   Under the FSMA 2000, s 168(2) the investigator has the power to require *any person* to attend before him at a specified time and place and answer questions, provide information and, in addition to ss 167 and 168(1), (4) powers, produce at a specified time and place any documents which appear to relate to any matter relevant to the investigation and give the investigator all assistance in connection with the investigation which he is reasonably able to give. The caveat in respect of *any person* is[1]:

'A person who is not the person under investigation or connected to that person may only be asked questions so long as the investigator is satisfied that it is necessary or expedient to do so.'

1   Explanatory Notes, p 67.

2.43 One possible justification for the broader powers under the FSMA 2000, s 168(2) is that there is a possibility of the offender being unknown at the commencement of the investigation. If this is the case then it would explain why it is that there is no requirement on the FSA to notify persons it intends to investigate under s 168(2) of its intention to do so. It does not deal satisfactorily with the subtle differences that exist under the sub-sections though, given that both sub-sections deal with investigations into substantive criminal offences that attract custodial sentences.

2.44 Irrespective of the applicable sub-section, the criteria for instigating appointment of investigators is not 'reasonable grounds to suspect' but 'circumstances suggesting'. It is submitted that this is a lower threshold than 'reasonable grounds' to overcome, and it is not in keeping with the spirit of the legislation that relies heavily on redress through judicial review.

Section 284 investigations

2.45 Section 284 investigations relate solely to the affairs of collective investment schemes. When considering whether to exercise its powers under the FSMA 2000, s 284 the FSA will have regard to the following factors:

- the seriousness of the matter;
- to what extent the interests of consumers are likely to be affected;
- whether the parties subject to the investigation are likely to co-operate with the FSA; and
- whether there are confidentiality obligations that may legitimately deter individuals from assisting the FSA.

2.46 The criteria for the appointment of an investigator is that it appears to the FSA that it is in the interests of participants or potential participants to investigate, or that the activities are a matter of public concern. Once appointed the investigator has the power to demand documents which appear to be under the control of the person subject to the investigation. The investigator may also demand the attendance of the person under investigation. Persons other than managers, trustees and operators of investment schemes will not generally be required to disclose information.

2.47 The requirement to supply documentary materials is supported by a power to apply for a warrant to enter and seize materials, if needed (FSMA 2000, s 176). The execution of the warrant must be by a constable. The Police and Criminal Evidence Act 1984 ('PACE 1984'), s 16 (execution of search warrants and safeguards) allows persons named on the warrant to accompany a constable for the purposes of execution of the warrant. This will clearly include FSA investigators.

2.48 The issue of banking confidentiality may well arise in respect of s 284 matters; these are specifically catered for under the FSMA 2000, s 175(5). Generally, material may not be requested unless one of four conditions is present:

- the person required to disclose is the person under investigation, or a member of the same group;
- confidentiality is owed to the person, or group member, who is under investigation;
- the person, or group member, under investigation consents to the disclosure; or
- the requirement to disclose has been specifically authorised by the FSA or the Secretary of State.

2.49 Section 284 investigatory powers are limited to those parties subject to the investigation. In this respect they mirror the '167' powers and do not extend to any person as covered by s 168 investigations. The power to request attendance before the investigator does not specify that the investigator may impose a location and time requirement; there is also no power under this section to demand answers to questions.

Challenges to FSA decision-making

2.50 This section comments on the avenues that exist to challenge the FSA when it decides to exercise its powers in respect of mainstream and peripheral criminal offending. There are a number of statutory defences contained within and outside of the FSMA 2000. These are subject to commentary in Chapter 3.

2.51 As a starting point to these discussions it is worth remembering that the FSA, as a body corporate, is immune from suit (FSMA 2000, Sch 1, para 19), except for actions taken in bad faith or in breach of the Human Rights Act 1998, s 6(1). It is a private company that discharges a public function and has now been in existence, de facto, since its change of name from the Securities and Investments Board in October 1997. Notwithstanding this unusual situation, there is an overall requirement on the FSA to exercise its powers with reasonableness.

2.52 Decisions of the FSA are subject to scrutiny by the Treasury, and there are four main powers that are contained within the FSMA 2000 to keep a check on FSA activities. First, the treasury may appoint or dismiss the FSA board and chairman. Second, the FSA must submit to the Treasury, at least once a year, a report covering the FSA's discharge of its functions. Third, the Treasury are empowered under the FSMA 2000, ss 12–18 to commission reviews and inquiries into the operations of the FSA. Fourth, the FSA is required to establish a complaints procedure that operates independently of the FSA. As a trade-off against further delay in its legislative passage, the government agreed to the proviso that there be the facility to appoint an independent investigator to review FSA decisions. In addition, this investigator has the authority to recommend compensation payments, made by the FSA, in cases of proven maladministration. An officer or employee of the FSA may not conduct an investigation of this nature on behalf of the independent investigator.

2.53 Part I and Sch 1 of the FSMA 2000 set out the requirements of the FSA's constitution. In essence these provisions require the FSA to conduct its affairs along the lines of generally accepted principles of good corporate governance. In pursuit of its public functions the FSA is subject not only to judicial review, but to the entire range of administrative law. It remains to be seen how successful judicial review will be in curbing any over zealous interpretations of the FSMA 2000 by the FSA, as there is a potential conflict. In a number of places throughout the FSMA 2000 the interpretation placed on the actions of an authorised person or his agent is subjective. That is, it is the subjective view of the FSA as to whether or not the action it has chosen to take is appropriate in the circumstances. This creates a dilemma, as it will be very difficult for the courts to determine that the actions of the FSA were unreasonable when the test for the reasonableness of the actions is based on the subjective view that the FSA is empowered to hold. On a more positive note, as the creation of FSA rules will be secondary legislation they are liable to be disapplied where it is impossible to interpret them in a way that is compatible with rights under the Human Rights Act 1998.

The role of the Tribunal

2.54 The Tribunal established under the FSMA 2000 is very different from that under the Financial Services Act 1986. The new Tribunal will sit regularly, is totally independent of the FSA and will be run by the Lord Chancellor's Department rather than the Treasury. The Tribunal has full first instance jurisdiction and has a primary responsibility to ensure that the FSA enforcement policies comply with art 6 of the European Convention on Human Rights ('ECHR') as well as ensuring that it (the Tribunal) is fully compliant with the Human Rights Act 1998. Matters brought before the Tribunal will be to contest the decisions of the FSA to issue decision notices and supervisory notices, typically where the FSA has decided to withdraw approval or authorisation or in cases where it has decided to impose a penalty.

2.55   Applicants have 28 days upon receipt of an FSA notice to lodge an appeal with the Tribunal. This period may be extended by the Tribunal and the FSA may not impose the restrictions appealed against during the period when the matter is being referred to the Tribunal. Matters brought before the Tribunal will be dealt with in public, and the Tribunal has legislative authority, under the FSMA 2000, s 133, to consider any evidence that it believes is relevant to the matter being considered. Persons may be summonsed to appear before the Tribunal and evidence is given on oath. Appeals against the decisions of the Tribunal, on a point of law only, are to the Court of Appeal.

2.56   As a general principle, market participants will not be able to rely on FSA guidance as a source of redress. However, there is the principle of legitimate expectation in that all persons subject to a law can reasonably expect that they will be told what the laws are that they are subject to and that those laws will be applied equally to all. In particular this doctrine extends to advice given by an arm or agency of the state. Section 119 of the FSMA 2000 stipulates that the FSA must prepare a Code to give guidance on whether or not, in the opinion of the FSA, behaviour amounts to market abuse. It will also give guidance on behaviour that does not, in the opinion of the FSA, amount to market abuse, and the Code may specify factors that are to be taken into account in determining whether such behaviour is or is not market abuse.

2.57   It is worth reflecting on the proposed scope of activity captured by market abuse. Market abuse will apply to the trading of securities, markets in commodity derivatives and financial futures. In this respect it is significantly broader than the activities captured by the offence of insider dealing under the Criminal Justice Act 1993, which applies to trading of securities only. It should be noted that it is the view of the FSA that the defences available under the insider dealing legislation are not replicated within the FSMA 2000, eg the insider dealing defence of not expecting to make a gain is not available under the FSMA 2000 for market abuse offences. This is made out on the basis that the preventative elements of the FSMA 2000 are what are important; that is preventing market abuse, not establishing whether an individual has made a financial gain.

2.58   The above is cited by way of example, and this does not exhaust the range of safe harbours that are available under the FSMA 2000; the remainder will be dealt with in detail in Chapter 3. It should be borne in mind that compliance with a rule is not an automatic exemption from liability. Many of the rules, including Listing Rules, cover matters outside of the scope of market abuse, and the establishment of safe harbours in a number of areas is still subject to discussion. The FSA is currently developing its strategy in respect of guidance, written and oral. Present thinking is that it would be persuasive evidence of compliance if, for example, oral guidance were sought from the FSA before executing a trade which subsequently were subject to action for a breach of the Code.

2.59   Provisions referred to in the Code may also take account of the City Code on Take-overs and Mergers to the effect that conformity with the City Code will be sufficient grounds to show that behaviour does not amount to market abuse. This provision has always been seen as contentious, and allowing the FSA to include City Code exemptions within the FSA's Code rather than the FSMA 2000 was decided by the narrowest of margins by the government when debated in parliament. The FSA has committed itself to a non-interventionist policy in take-over situations where the Panel on Take-overs and Mergers has all the requisite powers to act. The FSA may choose to intervene in cases of suspected market abuse. In such instances it submitted that the FSA will recognise that if a party has taken all reasonable steps that could be expected of him to show that he has complied with the guidance, and exercised those precautions and due diligence expected of a fit and proper person, further action would be suitable grounds for challenge.

2.60   Related to the concept in para **2.57** is that, in principle, public bodies may do anything that is not specifically prohibited by law. This must be viewed in the context of changing social expectations, for example, as has been seen in the interpretation of rights in respect of determining homosexuality as criminal in the UK. Thirty years ago there was no admissible issue under the ECHR. By 1982 attempts to criminalise acts between consenting adults, aged over 21 years, in private, were held to be a contravention of art 8 of the ECHR (*Dudgeon v United Kingdom*[1]). Consequently, legislative and executive powers must be exercised with proportionality.

1   (1981) 4 EHRR 149.

Reverse burden of proof

2.61   Contravention of a general prohibition is an offence. However, there is a defence provided that the defendant can show he took all reasonable precautions and exercised due diligence to avoid committing the offence (FSMA 2000, s 23(3)). A further example of a defence is contained within the FSMA 2000, s 25(2)(b), where again the onus of proof rests with the defendant to prove he took all reasonable precautions and exercised due diligence. It is arguable that these defences amount to a reverse burden of proof and are therefore subject to challenge.

2.62   The reverse burden of proof is generally offensive under adversarial legal systems and it is an established tenet of English law that a party is innocent until proven guilty. It is incumbent upon the prosecution to prove all elements of the allegation, and any statute that reverses the burden of proof is likely to fall foul of the Human Rights Act 1998. This position is not an absolute, but attempts to create a reversal of proof must be justifiable and subject to judicial scrutiny. In essence, any court will no doubt be cautious in sanctioning reverse onus legislation. The same principles must apply to the decision-making processes employed by the Tribunal also. In the decision of the Court of Appeal in *R v Lambert, Ali and Jordan*[1] the court differentiated between a persuasive burden and an evidential burden placed on the defendant. It was held that an evidential burden that rests with the defendant will generally be compatible with ECHR obligations; it would not generally be acceptable for a persuasive burden to be placed with the defendant.

1   [2001] 1 All ER 1014, [2001] 2 WLR 211.

2.63   The FSA has the power to investigate a broad range of criminal offences, within and external to the FSMA 2000. The Act provides for a number of statutory defences to criminal conduct, and the external legislation also has similar examples. Under the Code a number of safe harbours are created. Irrespective of whether the basis for the power is statutory or the Code, the FSA is accountable for its decision-making. The routes for challenge are both general and specific. Some are established principles enshrined within administration law and fundamental rights now protected under the Human Rights Act 1998, others are the specific creations of the FSMA 2000. The FSA has issued the following statement: 'The FSA's general policy is to pursue through the criminal justice system all those cases where criminal prosecution is appropriate'. The principles the FSA will apply to its decision-making process is the Code for Crown Prosecutors ('CPS'). It is submitted that the CPS Code is applicable to defined criminal conduct where standards of proof and public interest are of respectable antiquity. Few commentators seek to challenge the criminality of the offences to which the CPS Code applies. Many of the activities captured by the FSMA 2000 are new creations that have not previously been subject to penal sanctions. In some cases it is the very determination of the offence as criminal that will itself be the basis of challenge. The FSMA 2000 applies to a restricted class of persons, but should this be the basis for exceptional treatment by a unique body that has both regulatory and prosecutorial authority? How some of the tests and standards adopted will be applied in practice remains to be seen and challenged.

2.64   The recent decision in *Mahon v Rahn (No 2)*[1] may give some indication of the view that the courts are likely to take in respect of challenges on the basis of regulation being criminal in nature. In this case a firm of stockbrokers had been subject to a Serious Fraud Office ('SFO') investigation based on material supplied by the firm's bank to the Securities Authorisation Tribunal. The matters before the Tribunal were subject to an absolute privilege; the matter for the Court of Appeal to determine was whether or not this privilege extended to the letter sent by the firm's bank which was the basis for the SFO investigation. It was held that[2]:

'Important though the investigation of crime undoubtedly was, it was not possible to make a logical distinction between the situation in which a criminal investigator sought evidence to support a criminal charge and a situation in which a financial regulator sought evidence to put before a Tribunal to the effect that someone was not a fit and proper person to conduct investment business.'

The letter attracted absolute privilege.

1   [2000] 4 All ER 41, [2000] 1 WLR 2150, CA.
2   [2000] NLJR 899.

Complaints

2.65   For the purposes of completeness, a comment should be made about the provision for complaints against the FSA. Under the FSMA 2000 there is a two-part complaints scheme whereby challenges can be made in respect of complaints investigated by the FSA and complaints investigated independently. Matters relating to the discharge of FSA functions, other than legislative functions, will include maladministration, negligence, unreasonable delay, unprofessional behaviour, bias and lack of integrity. Any person or body corporate can challenge the FSA. Internal investigations will be conducted by a senior member of staff unconnected with the case. In the course of the investigation any findings of fact of a court of competent jurisdiction, the FSA Tribunal, or any other legally formed tribunal, will be conclusive evidence of the facts found.

2.66   Some complaints will be investigated by a Commissioner who will act independently of the FSA. His role will be to decide whether to investigate a matter referred to him, conduct a full and thorough enquiry, report his findings to the complainant and the FSA and publish a report. Discretion to investigate rests with the Commissioner. Further references to complaints as distinct from challenges can be found in 'Complaints Against the FSA, Draft Text for the FSA Handbook', Annex A and the FSMA 2000, Sch 1, paras 7 and 8.

summarily; six months' imprisonment and/or a fine up to the statutory maximum. Credit may arrive into an account from a theft or a money transfer obtained by deception.

1   Smith and Hogan *Criminal Law* (9th edn, 1999), p 55.

3.19   There is no offence of fraud under English law; therefore the offence most commonly charged is deception contrary to the Theft Act 1968. A deception can be committed deliberately or recklessly. A deception will be determined as deliberate if the defendant knows his statement is false or will or may be accepted as true by the victim. It is reckless if he is aware that it may be false and will or may be accepted as a truth by the victim. It is also reckless if the defendant is aware that his statement is ambiguous and may be taken by the victim to be true. As we have seen previously, if the defendant believes his statement to be true this will not amount to a deception; however, the more unreasonable his belief the more likely it is that a court or jury will be satisfied that the belief was not genuine. On this basis, if reference is made back to the Cunningham and Caldwell tests it can be seen that the Caldwell test is not applicable in respect of reckless statements. On conviction on indictment a person is liable to ten years' imprisonment. There is no statutory defence available under the Theft Act 1968.

3.20   For the purposes of completeness a brief mention needs to be made of the new insertion into the Theft Act 1968 of obtaining a money transfer by deception contrary to the FSMA 2000, s 15A. The offence was specifically created as a result of *R v Preddy*[1] and is restricted to the obtaining of money which does not extend in meaning to any securities. The offence is complete where a person obtains for himself or another, by any deception, a credit to one account and a debit from another where the credit results from the debit or the debit results from the credit.

On conviction on indictment a person is liable to ten years' imprisonment. There are no statutory defences available under this section.

1   [1995] Crim LR 564, CA.

Peripheral offences: sanctions and defences

3.21   This section will deal with the offences contained within Part XXVII of the FSMA 2000, except for matters where the primary legislation is other than the FSMA 2000, ie insider dealing, (market manipulation) and money laundering.

3.22   Carrying on a regulated activity without authorisation or exemption is a contravention of the general prohibition, referred to as an authorisation offence under the FSMA 2000. This is punishable with two years' imprisonment and/or an unlimited fine. If proceeded with at the magistrate's court the maximum sentence that may be imposed is six months' imprisonment and a fine of up to £5,000.

3.23 There is a statutory defence under the FSMA 2000, s 23(3) if the accused can prove that he exercised all due diligence and took all reasonable precautions to avoid committing the offence. Note the onus of proof is the civil standard, 'the balance of probabilities', and discharging the standard rests with the defence.

3.24 A person who is not authorised or exempt also commits an offence if he describes himself in any terms as an authorised person, if he describes himself as an exempt person or if he behaves in a manner which is reasonably likely to be understood to indicate that he is authorised or exempt (FSMA 2000, s 24). The same defence as under the FSMA 2000, s 23 exists, but it should be borne in mind that although onus of proof rests on the defendant it will be the 'reasonable man' test that is applicable in respect of the third offence listed (behaving in a manner to indicate that you are authorised or exempt). There is no mention of this under this section but any prudent market participant who inadvertently found themselves subject to prosecution under this limb would be well advised to be familiar with the accepted standards of behaviour that a regular market user (or reasonable man) would apply to the given facts.

3.25 The sentence range is the same as for the s 23 offence of carrying on without authorisation, that is up to two years' imprisonment on indictment and/or unlimited fine or six months' imprisonment and up to £5,000 fine if dealt with at the magistrate's court. In addition, if the holding oneself out to be authorised has included the use of any form of display or publicity, the sentence tariff will increase to include the maximum fine imposed multiplied by the number of days for which the display continued after receipt of a written notice from the FSA.

3.26 It is important to consider a difference that exists between the FSMA 2000 and the Explanatory Notes in respect of the display fine. Section 24(4) of the Act states that the fine will be 'multiplied by the number of days for which the display continued'. One interpretation that can be placed on this is that it means the multiplication fine will be applied from the date of receipt of notification to the effect that the display should not be used. The Explanatory Notes are less clear on this point and state that the applicable time is 'the number of days for which any material giving rise to the offence was on public display'. If the latter interpretation is applied by the courts then the relevant fine could be considerably more than if the words of the statute are applied. It is submitted that it is the statute that will apply and therefore the applicable date will be from receipt of notification.

Sanctions against inducements and invitations

3.27   There are a number of restrictions on financial promotions, and unauthorised persons are prohibited from issuing financial promotions in investment activities unless the content of the promotion is approved by an authorised person. There is a recognition under the FSMA 2000 that the fine line between 'cold calling' by telephone or by e-mail amounts to the same degree of intrusion on the investor, and a range of activities are captured by the provisions of s 21. These translate into an offence under s 25 where any person who breaches the financial promotion prohibition commits an offence and on conviction is liable to two years' imprisonment on indictment or six months at summary trial. The same range of fines applies as under s 23.

3.28   It is a defence, with the onus of proof on the defendant, to prove that he believed on reasonable grounds that (a) the content of the communication was prepared or approved by an authorised person, or that (b) he exercised due diligence and took reasonable precautions to avoid committing the offence. There is no requirement that all elements of the defence are proven, either (a) *or* (b) will suffice, but of note in respect to (b) is that there must be evidence of due diligence *and* taking reasonable steps.

Penalties for contravening Treaty rights

3.29   Misleading the FSA can amount to an offence under certain conditions. What is of note is that the offences covered in this section are clearly identified as criminal and they attract fines yet they do not attract custodial sentences. This presumably adds considerable weight to the continuing debate over the criminal nature of the market abuse regime when the penalty for market abuse mirrors those under Sch 4 of the FSMA 2000.

3.30   The FSMA 2000, Sch 4 gives effect to the rights of establishment of persons from other European Economic Area ('EEA') states. Treaty rights are not defined under the FSMA 2000, but the conditions for authorisation are set out and it is a requirement that any person or firm seeking to exercise a right under this Schedule must notify the FSA of its intention to do so. Failure to do this amounts to a criminal offence. It is also an offence to knowingly or recklessly provide false or misleading information.

3.31   Under para 5(2) of Sch 4 of the FSMA 2000 a firm must give at least seven days' notice of its intention to exercise Treaty rights. A contravention of s 5(2) is a criminal offence, and on summary conviction a person is liable to a fine not exceeding the statutory maximum. If convicted on indictment the fine is unlimited. It is a defence to prove that he took all reasonable precautions and exercised all due diligence to avoid committing the offence. Note the shift in burden of proof again and the use of the term 'reasonable'.

3.32 It is also an offence under Sch 4 when a person in, or in connection with, a notice given by him of his intention to exercise Treaty rights provides false or misleading information or is reckless in providing information that is false or misleading. There is no statutory defence to an offence under Sch 4, para 6(3). A person found guilty of an offence under this part is liable to an unlimited fine on indictment or the statutory maximum (£5,000) if dealt with at the magistrate's court.

3.33 There are no statutory defences in respect of intentionally or recklessly providing false or misleading information. It is, therefore, incumbent upon the prosecution to prove every element of the allegation to the requisite criminal standard. The FSMA 2000 is silent on the issue of intention, and being reckless has in itself been subject to considerable discussion in the criminal courts. Persons likely to be subject to a prosecution under this part of the FSMA 2000 will originate from another EEA state; this would seem a particularly good reason for clarity and defined legal expectations. Regrettably it would appear that this provision, as drafted, may suffer from a lack of precise meanings that can be attached to the criminal elements of the offence.

Intention and recklessness

3.34 The criminal law is rather unsettled in the area of intention, and judicial opinion has fluctuated over the years. In essence, since it is not possible to determine the contents of a person's mind we have to construct a sensible and workable approach towards identifying a person's intentions. This can be translated to mean that I intend an act if I act with the purpose of achieving a particular result. This will apply whether I am actually capable of achieving that desired outcome or not. This view has been commented upon by Professor Sir John Smith in the leading criminal law text Smith and Hogan *Criminal Law*[1] (9th edn, 1999). What Smith proposes is a two-stage approach to identifying intention: first, a result is intended when it is the actor's purpose to cause it; second, a court or jury may also find (note the term *may* rather than *will* or *must*) that a result is intended, although it was not the actor's purpose to cause it when (a) the result is a virtual certainty of that act, and (b) the actor knows that it is a virtually certain consequence[1]. Regrettably this is not the full extent of the debate, as intention does not have the same meaning for all offences.

1   Smith and Hogan *Criminal Law* (9th edn, 1999), p 55.

3.35 The actions of a person will not always be intended, and there are many examples under the FSMA 2000 where the law seeks to legislate against the reckless acts of a market participant. Most commonly a person will be determined as reckless if he takes an unjustifiable risk that causes a particular event. The criminal law has developed two streams of recklessness, Cunningham and Caldwell, named after the respective criminal cases.

Cunningham recklessness requires proof that the defendant was aware of an unjustifiable risk. Caldwell is satisfied if either the defendant was aware of the risk or, in the case of an obvious risk, he failed to give any thought to the possibility of the existence of the risk. Some offences require proof of Cunningham recklessness, others require proof of Caldwell.

3.36   For the purposes of the criminal offences that may be investigated and prosecuted by the FSA, the applicable recklessness test is not certain. For example, for those criminal acts that contain dishonesty there should be no need for any recklessness test. However, some regulatory offences dealt with before the establishment of the FSA have been subject to a Caldwell test, eg *Data Protection Registrar v Amnesty International*[1].

1   [1995] Crim LR 633.

3.37   The application of the relevant evidential criteria is at present uncharted territory. The most probable way forward will be to utilise the application to recklessness that is given to deception offences, as this is one area in which the FSA is likely to identify criminal conduct. A deception is reckless if the defendant is aware that the representation may be false or may be accepted as true, or if he is aware that it is ambiguous. On this basis it is clear as to what would amount to a reckless statement being made to an appointed inspector, the FSA or the Department of Trade and Industry.

3.38   If the defendant believes his statement to be true, he is not reckless, even if his belief is unreasonable. However, the more unreasonable his alleged belief, the more likely it is that a court or jury will be satisfied that the belief was not genuine. It is submitted that this line of reasoning, proposed by Prof Smith, will be that adopted in respect of reckless statements made under the FSMA 2000. For further commentary see Smith and Hogan *Criminal Law* (9th edn, 1999).

Fit and proper

3.39   Under Part V of the FSMA 2000 the FSA has a range of powers to ensure that persons are fit and proper to perform their functions within the financial marketplace. This Part is aimed at employees of authorised firms and, where relevant, to bodies corporate. An example cited in the Explanatory Notes (at p 33) is where a life assurance company enters into an arrangement with a firm of estate agents to sell life assurance. The agency and staff would need approval before giving investment advice. Also mentioned are the now commonplace arrangements in larger multinationals where 'matrix managers' carry out a range of functions for associated companies within the group. The FSA is empowered to ensure that managers in such positions are fit and proper.

3.40   The FSMA 2000, s 56 allows the FSA to make an order that prohibits any person it deems to be unfit from engaging in authorised activities. The order may be all-inclusive or it may prohibit a specified function. Failure to conform with an order is a criminal offence. The offence is complete when a person either performs, or agrees to perform, a function in breach of an order. This offence is triable at the magistrate's court only and is subject to a maximum sanction of level 5 (£5,000). This offence is a further example under the FSMA 2000 of a criminal offence that attracts a non-custodial sanction. It is the nature of the sentence that determines the status of the offence and, in this instance, it should in no way detract from the fact that defendants are entitled to the full protection of the criminal law.

3.41   There is a defence under s 56(5) if a person can show that he took all reasonable precautions and exercised all due diligence to avoid performing or agreeing to perform. Onus of proof, again, rests with the defendant. Note the inclusiveness of the defence in that a person must prove he took reasonable precautions *and* exercised due diligence. In reality this rather limits the opportunity for a successful defence of the first limb as it would be very difficult to discharge the burden of proof to the effect that a participant is performing a particular regulated function but nevertheless took all reasonable precautions and exercised all due diligence to ensure that he was not acting in breach of an order, when it is a statutory requirement that the FSA precedes an order with a warning notice.

Listing particulars and prospectuses: punishments and defences

3.42   Under the FSMA 2000 it is a requirement that listing particulars are lodged with the Registrar of Companies on or before the date on which they are published (s 84). If the issuer of the securities in question, or any person who is party to the publication, fails to comply with this requirement, it is an offence punishable with a fine up to the statutory maximum of £5,000 or an unlimited fine on indictment (s 84(3)). There is no statutory defence available under the FSMA 2000.

3.43   It is a requirement under the Listing Rules that a prospectus must be published before securities are offered to the public in the UK. What amounts to being offered to the public is covered under s 103(6) and Sch 11 of the FSMA 2000; for example if the offer is being made to less than 50 persons it is not offered for the purposes of the Act. If a prospectus is required to be published then any offer of new securities to a person before publication will amount to a criminal offence. A person found guilty of this offence is liable to three months' imprisonment on summary conviction or a fine not exceeding £5,000 and on conviction on indictment to two years' imprisonment and/or an unlimited fine (FSMA 2000, s 85(3)). There is no statutory defence available. It will not be deemed an offence if the prospectus itself does not comply with the rules in respect of content and form.

Issuing advertisements without authority

3.44   In its overall responsibility towards protecting the consumers of financial products the FSA will approve, and then authorise, the contents of the advertising of products. Without such authority no advertisement or other information may be released. This offence only applies where listing particulars are, or are to be, published. A contravention of this provision will render a person liable to a fine up to the statutory maximum at the magistrate's court and imprisonment of up to two years and/or an unlimited fine on indictment. It is a slightly unusual sentence range as it is usually the case that if a custodial sentence is attracted this will be applicable summarily and on indictment. This is not the case under the FSMA 2000, s 98(2).

3.45   There is a statutory defence in that a person will not be liable where he reasonably believed that the advertisement had been approved or its issue had been authorised by the competent authority. This can be translated to mean that if a person has advertised on the instructions of another party who he has reason to believe has authority then this will suffice for the purposes of this defence. There is also a safe harbour in respect of civil liability to the effect that if authority is granted this will be evidence that the information or advertisement does not mislead (FSMA 2000, s 98 (4)).

Section 177 offence: sanctions and defences

3.46   The power to order the production of information and documents and to instigate investigations is within Part XI of the FSMA 2000. Under s 177 of the Act a failure to comply with any of the range of requirements available to the FSA or the appointed investigator will amount to a criminal offence. The range of requirements applicable has been detailed in previous paragraphs (see paras **3.42** and **3.43**) and includes a power to require information, order reports by skilled persons, appoint persons to carry out general and specific investigations, and conduct investigations on behalf of overseas regulators. Any failure to comply with any of the entire range of requirements, without a reasonable excuse, renders the person liable to six months' imprisonment or a fine up to the statutory maximum.

3.47   Caution should be exercised at this point as the Explanatory Notes are not a model of clarity. The matters referred to at para 346 of the Notes are in connection with preventing the execution of a warrant for which the penalty is three months' imprisonment and/or a fine. The other offences captured under s 177, typically knowingly or recklessly providing false information, attract six months and/or a fine on summary conviction and up to two years, and/or an unlimited fine, on indictment.

3.48   Under s 177(3) it is a defence to the range of offences captured (including, for example, concealing and falsifying information) if the defendant can show he had no intention of concealing facts from the investigator. This introduces another concept from the established criminal law, which is intent. Like recklessness, intention has been the subject of considerable case law commentary and its inclusion in the FSMA 2000 will perhaps only add confusion to an already complex Act. The onus of proof rests with the defendant, and therefore it would be safe to proceed on the basis that the intention will be subjective; that is not as viewed by the 'reasonable man' but by the defendant himself. As with all evidential burdens that rest with the defence, the standard of proof to be discharged is to the civil standard, the balance of probabilities.

3.49   A further offence under s 177 would be to intentionally obstruct a person who is executing a warrant issued under this part of the FSMA 2000. This offence can only be heard at the magistrate's court and on conviction a person is liable to a maximum of three months' imprisonment and/or a fine up to level 5 on the standard scale (currently £5,000).

Control over authorised persons: punishments and defences

3.50   Part XII of the FSMA 2000 deals with two main themes: persons who intend to exercise control over an authorised person by virtue of their voting or shareholder rights, and any increase or decrease in the amount of control a person has over an authorised person. Section 191 of the FSMA 2000 specifies the criminal offences that can be committed. The first offence of failing to notify the FSA of proposed acquisition, increase or reduction in control is punishable by a fine not exceeding the statutory maximum that can be imposed at the magistrate's court. This offence is not triable on indictment.

3.51   It is also an offence to proceed with an acquisition, reduction or increase in control without FSA permission. This offence has been discussed in detail in Chapter 2; the important point being that the FSA has three months from the date of receipt of a notification to respond. During this three-month period a person cannot proceed with the proposed changes. If he does then it is an offence punishable with a fine up to the statutory maximum; again this offence is triable summarily only.

3.52   There are a number of offences contained within the FSMA 2000, s 191 around the subject of notification of proposed changes in control. The majority are summary offences only that attract fines and not custodial sentences. Under sub-s (5) there is a more serious offence that, on conviction, can result in two years' imprisonment and an unlimited fine. In addition, this offence – acquiring control when there is an FSA warning notice in force at the time – is liable to an additional fine of up to one-tenth of the statutory maximum, ie £50 per day, every day on which the offence has continued (FSMA 2000, s 191(8)).

3.53   There is a statutory defence available, but it has a limited application. If a person is charged with the offence of failing to notify a proposed acquisition, reduction or increase in control, it is a defence to show (the onus of proof is on the defendant) that he had no knowledge of the act or circumstances by which a duty to notify the FSA arose. However, this defence is limited in scope because at the point in time that he does become aware of the need to notify the FSA, if he then fails to do so within 14 days the defence is not applicable. And this failure to notify in itself now becomes an offence punishable with a fine up to the statutory maximum at the magistrate's court.

There is no statutory defence to the more serious offence of acquiring control whilst an FSA warning notice is in force.

Director General of Fair Trading prosecutions

3.54   Under certain circumstances, the FSA and the Director General of Fair Trading have authority to be involved in matters relating to the business of 'incoming firms', ie EEA and Treaty firms. This authority is referred to as the power of intervention and is contained within Part XIII of the FSMA 2000. The Director General of Fair Trading has the power under the FSMA 2000 to issue a consumer credit prohibition notice to a firm. He may also issue a consumer credit restriction if he believes that the notice has not been complied with. Prohibitions may be absolute or conditional. Restrictions may be withdrawn or subject to variation. Proceedings for the offence of failing to comply with a notice requirement may be instigated by the Director General of Fair Trading as well as the FSA. Proceedings in a matter of contravening a restriction order may only be brought by the FSA.

3.55   Contravention of a notice or restriction order is a criminal offence punishable with a fine up to the statutory maximum if heard at the magistrate's court, or an unlimited fine if dealt with on indictment. This is a further example of a criminal offence under the FSMA 2000 where imprisonment is not an option available to the courts. There are no statutory defences to either matter available under the FSMA 2000.

Professional body exemptions

3.56   The provision of financial services by some professionals is now well established. This is viewed as an ancillary service and under specific circumstances it is possible to gain exemption from the FSA to carry out certain regulated activities. The arrangements for general exemptions that apply to a member of a professional body are contained within Part XX of the FSMA 2000. There are eight designated professional bodies and they are listed on p 22 of the Glossary of Definitions, Consultation Paper 65a.

3.57 Making a false claim to be exempt is an offence. Behaving or indicating to another that one is exempt is an offence. In addition, if the conduct constituting the offence involved the public display of any material, this is also an offence. All of these offences are triable at the magistrate's court only. The sanction for making a false claim is a maximum of six months' imprisonment and/ or a fine up to the statutory limit. Behaving or indicating that one is exempt has the same sentence tariffs as making a false claim. If one has also committed the public displaying of material offence, this is liable to a fine of up to the statutory maximum multiplied by the number of days for which the display continued.

3.58 There are two issues of note here. First, the Explanatory Notes state that in respect of the display offence the time period will be 'the number of days for which any material giving rise to the offence was on public display'[1]. The FSMA 2000 says that the period will be the number of days for which the display continued. Whilst it is attractive to suggest that a sensible and purposeful interpretation of the statute would suggest that it is from when the material was on public display, this may be financially prejudicial to a defendant who is seeking for the interpretation of the law to be from that period in time when he was notified to the effect that he would be subject to a prosecution. This could be some considerable time after the material had been on public display and would therefore attract a significantly less fine multiplier. This is a severe sanction by any standards; by comparison we have seen in para **3.57** that acquiring control whilst a notice is in force will attract a daily fine of up to one-tenth of the statutory maximum. This would appear to be a further example of sentencing disparity under the FSMA 2000.

1   Explanatory Notes, p 110.

Penalties for misleading an auditor or actuary

3.59 It is an offence for an authorised person (or his officer, controller or manager) to knowingly or recklessly give false or misleading information to an auditor or actuary. On summary conviction he is liable to imprisonment not exceeding six months and/or a fine up to the statutory limit. On indictment he is liable to two years' imprisonment and/or an unlimited fine. Auditor or accountant means one appointed under the FSMA 2000 or as a result of a provision contained in rules. The prosecution will have to discharge the same evidential burdens in respect of recklessness as discussed previously, but there are no specific statutory defences available.

Penalties for disclosing information

3.60 There are three categories dealt with under Part XXIII disclosing information that is held by a primary recipient, disclosing information that is in the possession of the Inland Revenue and disclosing competition information. The FSMA 2000, s 352 deals with the first two and s 351 of the Act with competition matters.

3.61 There are two offences related to primary recipient information and two offences related to Inland Revenue information. Under the FSMA 2000 it is recognised that the FSA will have access to confidential information, and it is essential that this information is not disclosed inappropriately. Information is deemed confidential unless it is in the public domain or it is not possible to ascertain the individual identity of the particular person to whom the information relates. These limitations do not amount to statutory defences; it is simply the case that if these points were proven at an early stage in an investigation there would be no point in continuing and a prosecution would not be pursued. This offence is mirrored in respect of information held by the Inland Revenue where it will be an offence to disclose information it holds unless it is disclosed by the Inland Revenue or in accordance with the FSMA 2000, s 350(4)(c), (d). What this tells us is that information may be disclosed if it is in connection with an FSA investigation into any of the criminal offences legislated against under the FSMA 2000 as well as those the FSA has authority to investigate that are contained in other legislation, ie insider dealing and money laundering.

The penalty for disclosing either confidential information or Inland Revenue information is imprisonment not exceeding three months and/or a fine up to the statutory maximum at summary trial, two years and/or an unlimited fine on indictment.

3.62 Further offences are committed if a person who is in possession of confidential information uses it. The same proviso applies in respect of the use of Inland Revenue information. These matters are triable summarily only and consequently have a maximum imprisonment tariff of three months and/or a fine up to level 5.

3.63 There is one statutory defence that applies to all the offences mentioned. It is a defence for the accused to prove that he did not know, and had no reason to believe, that the information was confidential, and that he took all reasonable precautions and exercised all due diligence to avoid committing the offence.

3.64 Under the FSMA 2000, s 351 it is an offence to disclose competition information. As with the offences under ss 348 and 350(5) of the Act, the relevant terminological definitions are specified in the actual sections. Under this limb if a person has competition information that relates to the affairs of an individual who is still alive, or a company that is still trading, and he improperly discloses, it is an offence punishable with a fine up to the statutory limit at the magistrate's court (note no custodial sentence) and two years' imprisonment and/or an unlimited fine on indictment. There are no statutory defences available.

3.65 As seen previously, the matter will not proceed to trial if a disclosure is made with the consent of the person or company concerned or if it is to assist with criminal proceedings. Interestingly, a disclosure is not improper when made in connection with the investigation of any criminal offence triable in the UK. This provision is considerably wider than that in respect of disclosing under the FSMA 2000, ss 348 or 350(5), presumably because it is felt that to inhibit competition is not only domestically disadvantageous but also because it may infringe upon EC laws. Nevertheless *any* criminal offence is particularly inclusive, and it does seem rather curious to think that it would not be improper to disclose sensitive competition information during a public hearing into a speeding offence.

Voluntary liquidation: prohibitions, sanctions and defences

3.66 The FSA has two interests in the area of liquidations: implications for customers when an insurance firm becomes insolvent, and the regulatory process of winding up in response to the precursory events. As a result of a number of high-profile cases throughout the past decade, an insurance company that effects long-term policies, or life assurance, may not enter into voluntary liquidation without the consent of the FSA (FSMA 2000, s 366). This provision does not create an absolute prohibition on winding up, but seeks to ensure that the FSA is involved in the entire regulatory process throughout. The primary thrust of the provisions is to ensure that the interests of policy holders are secured and confidence in the financial sector is maintained.

3.67 A person who fails to notify the FSA of his intentions to propose a resolution for voluntary winding up commits an offence. On summary conviction he is liable to a fine not exceeding the statutory limit. This offence does not attract a custodial sentence and may only be dealt with at the magistrate's court. There is no statutory defence available, but reference should be made to the FSMA 2000, s 366(4), which specifies the provisions that do not apply in relation to a winding-up resolution. It is a further requirement of the section that if and when the FSA consents to winding up it will issue a certificate. This certificate must accompany the paperwork sent to the Registrar of Companies. Failure to do so is not an offence, but the winding-up resolution will be treated as having no effect.

Sanctions against misleading investigators, the FSA and the Tribunal

3.68 The offences legislated against in this part are arguably the most important and serious to be considered under peripheral offences. In particular, this part deals with making false statements and dishonestly concealing facts. The severity of the matter is reflected in the sentence tariffs that are more severe than any others seen so far. For creating a false or misleading impression a person is liable, on indictment, to seven years' imprisonment.

3.69   A further reflection of this severity is that the offences of misleading or concealing facts can be committed by any person, whether an authorised person or not. The fact that the term 'dishonestly' is employed in this provision does invite reference, once again, to the established criminal law. If the provisions of the Theft Act 1968 are utilised then what is dishonest is set against what society expects of an honest person. In this respect the Theft Act 1968 is quite specific and the actions of honest people have now been well articulated in the courts. It would be sensible to attach the same meaning to dishonesty as understood under the Theft Act.

3.70   There are two offences: deliberately making misleading statements or dishonestly concealing facts, and making a misleading statement with the intention of inducing someone to act upon the statement. This is commonly referred to as 'market manipulation'. The offence of inducing someone is not committed unless the action done takes place in the UK or the misleading impression created arises in the UK.

Both offences attract maximum sentences in the magistrate's court: up to six months' imprisonment and/or a fine up to the statutory limit. Both offences are punishable with up to seven years' imprisonment and/or an unlimited fine on indictment.

3.71   There is one statutory defence to making false statements or concealing facts. It is a defence for him to show that the statement, promise or forecast was made in conformity with price stabilising rules or control of information rules.

There are three statutory defences to the inducing offence. In all instances the burden of proof rests with the defendant. It is a defence that he reasonably believed his act or conduct would not create a false or misleading impression. The second defence is that he acted or engaged in such conduct for the purposes of stabilising the price of investments and in conformity with price stabilising rules. The third defence is that he acted or engaged in the conduct in conformity with the control of information rules.

3.72   Under the FSMA 2000, s 398 it is a criminal offence if you supply false or misleading information to the FSA. This provision captures matters that are not already subject to sanctions elsewhere under the FSMA 2000; for example there is the specific offence of supplying misleading information to an inspector appointed under s 177.

3.73   Matters dealt with in Part XI can be heard summarily or on indictment; the maximum sentences applicable are fines to the standard scale limit and an unlimited fine respectively. There are no statutory defences available. There is a requirement that it is shown that the defendant acted knowingly or recklessly.

3.74 The final criminal sanction applicable under Part IV relates to the work of the Tribunal. The Tribunal has the authority to demand the attendance of any person and produce any document it considers necessary. A person who, without reasonable excuse, fails to attend or give evidence commits an offence and is liable on summary conviction to a fine not exceeding the maximum.

3.75 It is also an offence to alter, suppress, conceal or destroy a document required by the Tribunal. This is viewed as a more serious offence. At summary trial the offence does not attract imprisonment; the sanction is a fine up to the statutory maximum. However, on indictment the penalty is up to two years' imprisonment and/or an unlimited fine. There are no statutory defences available under the FSMA 2000.

3.76 It is accepted that the purpose of the Explanatory Notes is to provide an overview. Nevertheless, it is again appropriate to alert users to the fact that no mention is made of the actions that will constitute committing the more serious offence that attracts a potential custodial tariff of two years' imprisonment.

Insider dealing: defences and penalties

Defences

3.77 Under Part V of the Criminal Justice Act 1993 ('CJA 1993') there are a range of statutory defences. These can be usefully divided into two parts: general defences and specific defences.

General defences are contained within s 53 of the CJA 1993; specific defences are in Sch 1 of the CJA 1993.

3.78 The FSMA 2000 pattern of shifting the burden of proof onto the defendant is also apparent under the general defences in the CJA 1993, where throughout the burden of proof rests firmly with the defendant, to the now familiar standard of 'on the balance of probabilities'. There are three mainstream offences under the CJA 1993: dealing, encouraging and disclosing. Not all of the defences apply to all the offences.

3.79 It is a defence for the defendant to show that he did not anticipate any person making a profit or loss to derive from his dealing. This defence is applicable to all three offences. The key element here is clearly the mind of the defendant, and the court will seek to be satisfied that the motive behind this dealing was not to make a gain or cause a loss.

3.80   The second general defence applies to dealing and encouraging only. It is a defence to show that at the time of the dealing or encouraging the defendant believed, on reasonable grounds, that the information had been disclosed. The purpose of this provision is to ensure that market participants are not prejudiced by a lack of information. There are two elements to the defence: belief and reasonable grounds for holding that belief. Successfully discharging this evidential burden will entail convincing the court that the belief held is an honest belief and reasonable under the circumstances. This can be translated to mean: would a reasonable person, in the defendant's position, have arrived at the conclusion held by the defendant? It would not suffice for the defendant alone to hold that he felt his belief was reasonable.

3.81   The third general defence applies to dealing and encouraging, not disclosing. This defence applies when a person can show that he would have done what he did whether he was in possession of the information or not. In other words, he is saying that the information had no effect on the course of action taken. The motive of the defendant will again play a crucial role in discharging the evidential burden, and courts will look for corroborative evidence of a tangible nature to support the alleged innocent state of mind, eg where shares have to be sold notwithstanding the possession of inside information[1].

1   See Rider, BAK and Ashe, M *Insider Crime* (1993).

3.82   The fourth general defence applies to disclosing only. It is a defence to show that he did not expect any person to deal because of the disclosure. This applies to *any* person dealing, not just the person to whom the disclosure was made. This defence is in addition to the first outlined in para **3.79** where a person can show that he did not expect a loss or profit to result from the dealing.

Specific defences

3.83   These defences can be altered or amended by the Treasury as they are specifically designed to take account of applicable market conditions. Under the CJA 1993, Sch 1 there are defences that relate to market makers, price stabilisation and market information. Market information is sub-divided into acting on market information, acquisitions and disposals.

Market makers

3.84   It will not amount to an offence of insider dealing if a defendant market maker can show that he acted in good faith in the course of his business. The CJA 1993 describes what amounts to a market maker under para 1 of Sch 1. There is no requirement that the information obtained was acquired in the course of business; the emphasis is that ' ... the market makers should be able to continue to quote two-way continuous prices as long as they act in good faith'[1].

1   Parliamentary Debates, House of Commons Standing Committee B, 15 June 1993, col 126.

Price stabilisation

3.85   It is a defence to a charge of insider dealing to show that the defendant was acting in conformity with price stabilising rules. Price stabilising rules for the purposes of the CJA 1993 are defined in Sch 1, para 5(2). There are practical limitations to this defence, and unless it can be shown that there has been conformity with the specific rules then there is no defence; eg the rules only apply to certain types of investments, defined as 'relevant securities', and the stabilising period must be operative.

Market information

3.86   Market information is defined under the CJA 1993, Sch 1, para 4 as one or more of the following:

- securities of a particular kind are or have been acquired or disposed of, or their acquisition or disposal is under consideration or is the subject of negotiation;
- securities of a particular kind have not been, or are not to be, acquired or disposed of;
- the number of securities acquired or disposed of, or to be acquired or disposed of, their acquisition or disposal is under consideration or is the subject of negotiation;
- the range of prices at which securities have been or are to be acquired or disposed of is under consideration or is the subject of negotiation;
- the identity of the persons involved or likely to be involved in the above; and
- it is a defence to show that the defendant acted reasonably with the information that he had despite the fact that the information was inside information at the time. The use of 'reasonably' should be interpreted as being an objective test. That is, what would a market participant in his position in compliance with the relevant rules be likely to do in the circumstances?

3.87   A second defence in contravention of the market information offence is provided where the defendant can show that he acted in connection with or in the course of a series of such acquisitions or disposals and his actions were with a view to facilitating the acquisition or disposal, and the information in his possession was market information arising directly out of his involvement in the acquisition or disposal. These are not mutually exclusive and all three provisions must be proven, by the defendant, if the defence is to apply.

3.88   The penalty for insider dealing following conviction on indictment is up to seven years' imprisonment and/or an unlimited fine. On summary conviction the penalty is up to six months' imprisonment and/or a fine not exceeding the statutory maximum.

Money laundering

3.89   We have seen previously that there is an area of potential overlap between the powers to investigate and prosecute offences of handling stolen goods and instances when the goods referred to is money derived from criminal conduct. It may be advantageous for the FSA to support a prosecution under the Money Laundering Regulations (SI 1993/1933) as these may more accurately reflect the degree of involvement and offences committed than charging handling stolen goods.

3.90   The inclusion of money laundering within the scope of the investigations that may be conducted by the FSA reflects the regulatory role of the FSA as under the FSMA 2000 there are a few subtle, but relevant, extensions beyond the existing law. For example, by implication all staff have a responsibility to report suspicions, and this is translated as a strict liability placed on firms regardless of the reporting measures they have attempted to put in place. In addition, it is recognised that there may be circumstances under which it would be difficult to obtain the normal identity-checking documents, such as passports or driving licences, from individuals. Rule 3.3.5 of the Money Laundering Regulations 1993 allows firms to overcome this problem by permitting the use of other evidence. Some market participants may be justified in thinking that the existing regime was sufficient; nevertheless, the FSMA 2000 has added a further layer to those provisions already in place.

3.91   There are two classes of offences applicable to those in the financial service industry. First, the specific provisions under the Money Laundering Regulations 1993. A failure to take appropriate measures to prevent money laundering under the 1993 Regulations, for example not reporting, is punishable with up to two years' imprisonment and/or an unlimited fine on indictment, and on summary conviction a fine up to the statutory limit. The second category of offending is general to the entire population and captures the more serious offences of actively assisting in or taking measures to prevent the identification of those involved in money laundering. These offences are those commonly referred to as assisting, using, concealing and tipping-off. The penalty for conviction on indictment for all of these offences is a term of imprisonment not exceeding 14 years and/or an unlimited fine. If dealt with summarily, they carry a term of imprisonment not exceeding six months and/or a fine up to the statutory maximum. There are statutory defences to assisting, using and tipping off. There is no statutory defence to concealing or transferring the proceeds of criminal conduct. (Criminal Justice Act 1988, s 93C).

Defences

3.92 It is a defence, under the Money Laundering Regulations 1993, reg 5(4), for any of the proceedings brought under the 1993 Regulations to show that the defendant took all reasonable steps and exercised all due diligence to avoid committing the offence.

Assisting

3.93 Under the Criminal Justice Act 1988, s 93A it is a defence (with the burden of proof on the defendant) to show that he did not know or suspect that the arrangement was for the purposes of laundering the proceeds of criminal conduct, or that he intended to disclose his suspicion but had a reasonable excuse for failing to do so. The test for reasonable suspicion is subjective (ie the defendant will have to prove to the court that the belief he held was reasonable); it is not what is reasonable by the standards of the ordinary man. In order to encourage the reporting of suspicions, there is legal immunity against actions under breach of contract where disclosures are made. The Court of Appeal laid down guidelines relating to situations where a firm receives a court order to disclose documents, but in doing so it will commit an offence under the money laundering legislation. Reference should be made to *C v S*[1].

1   [1999] 2 All ER 343, [1999] 1 WLR 1551, CA.

Using

3.94 This offence requires the prosecution to prove that the defendant knew the property in question to be directly or indirectly the proceeds of crime. Suspicion or belief that the property is such will not suffice for the purposes of a prosecution. It is a defence if the person who acquires, uses or possesses the property has provided adequate consideration. The test of adequate consideration is not stated; instead the Act states that a person uses or has possession of property for inadequate consideration if the value of the consideration is significantly less than the value of his use or possession of the property (CJA 1993, s 93B(4)). There is a further defence if the defendant acted with the prior consent of the police, or if he intended to report his suspicions to the police but had a reasonable excuse for failing to do so.

3.95 The burden of proof appears to shift under this section. It is for the defendant to prove that he has given adequate consideration. It is for the defendant to prove that he intended to inform the police but had a reasonable excuse for failing to do so. It is for the prosecution to disprove that when a disclosure is made after the Act, but on the defendant's own initiative, it was not made as soon as it was reasonable for the defendant to do so.

3.96 Intriguingly, under the CJA 1993, s 93B(2) it is possible that a person may succeed with the defence of adequate consideration even in cases where the defendant was aware that the property concerned represents the proceeds of crime.

Tipping off

3.97 Disclosing information that is potentially prejudicial to an investigation into money laundering is commonly referred to as 'tipping off'. It is for the prosecution to prove that the defendant knew or suspected that an investigation was being, or was about to be, conducted. There is no attempt under the legislation to limit bona fide legal advice, other than that in this respect it is a specific defence (onus of proof on the defendant) to show that he did not know or suspect that the disclosure was likely to be prejudicial.

3.98 It follows that this offence is complete even though it may not be the intention of the defendant to prejudice enquiries or prevent the detection of money laundering offences. If a disclosure is made that is thoughtless or unsolicited it will still constitute commission of the offence, and it will then be for the defendant to successfully raise a statutory defence.

3.99 The key words 'knowledge' and 'suspicion' are used in a number of the offences outlined above, in particular with respect to money laundering. Knowledge is essentially a question for the jury to determine on the basis that it would be reasonable for a jury to ask itself why it was that the defendant did not draw certain inferences from another person's actions or behaviour. However, it may present an interesting dilemma for any jury to determine that a defendant acted in a deliberate manner if they are negligent in failing to draw conclusions from a sequence of events rather than deliberate in turning a blind eye to the obvious.

3.100 Given the potential problems that might be encountered in determining knowledge, there is the alternative element of mens rea: suspicion. There is considerable emphasis within the legislation and under the FSMA 2000 to encourage staff to report suspicions of money laundering. However, suspicion is a difficult state of mind to determine, and the distinction between being satisfied that a transaction does not amount to money laundering and believing the same may be hard to establish. On this basis it is potentially easier to inadvertently commit the offence of assisting than the other offences captured by the money laundering provisions.

Conclusion

3.101   All of the offences referred to above are punishable with a fine and, in many instances, a defendant may be imprisoned if found guilty. As such the sanctions are criminal and all defendants should be entitled to the full protection of the law with the same rights as any other citizen who is subject to a criminal investigation. The incorporation of the European Convention on Human Rights into our legislative order under the Human Rights Act 1998 means that it will no longer be necessary to take matters such as the right to a fair trial or the protection of one's private life to Strasbourg. The FSMA 2000 applies to any actions taken by a court or Tribunal regardless of whether the act is public or private in nature.

3.102   The FSMA 2000 provides for a legal aid scheme which implies a recognition of the criminal nature of the sanctions and acknowledges the fundamental human right to a fair trial. There are a number of evidential issues that have yet to be satisfactorily resolved, and the dilemmas created are explored in Chapter 5. For the purposes of punishments and defences, we can expect the FSA to use the full range of options available to it to detect and prevent criminal offending within the financial service sector. Many of these powers have been questioned during the Committee stages of the FSMA 2000. Not all the answers supplied by the government have reduced the concerns held. There is little comfort to be found in the defences as a reliance on established criminal law may only highlight the areas of existing confusion. The FSA can anticipate a number of challenges being brought before the Tribunal and the UK courts, before the entire range of terminological meanings and defences are established in compliance with the Human Rights Act 1998.

CHAPTER 4

Investigations by other agencies

4.1   The Financial Services Authority ('FSA') has statutory authority to instigate and prosecute a number of criminal offences. In reality it is unlikely that it will proceed with high profile criminal investigations in isolation, and over the course of the next few years market participants can expect to see joint investigations and prosecutions brought by, amongst others, the FSA, the Crown Prosecution Service ('CPS'), and the Serious Fraud Office ('SFO') where the initial investigation has been conducted by any one of a number of agencies. In this chapter the relationship that is likely to develop between the FSA and other agencies is explored, as well as an overview of the role of the other principal enforcement agencies in the field of financial crime.

4.2   It has become clear in Chapters 1–3 that criminal investigations are frequently conducted as a result of suspected regulatory transgressions. In this chapter it is the role of the criminal investigation agencies that is discussed; however, the role of agencies such as the Department of Trade and Industry ('DTI'), the Director General of Fair Trading ('DGFT'), HM Customs and Excise and the Inland Revenue is also considered as there is potentially considerable overlap between the functions of these departments and the work of the FSA in respect of the gathering of information and subsequent use of evidence obtained in a civil inquiry for the purposes of a criminal prosecution.

Investigations by the police

4.3   There are 43 mainstream police forces in the UK and, consequently, the degree of attention and resources directed towards preventing and detecting financial crimes is sporadic. The greatest intensity of activity is centred around the capital and principal cities. All police forces are required to maintain an office for the investigation of commercial crimes, but in some cases the department may be located within mainstream criminal investigations and the detachment of staff can be as few as one. This is not the picture in London where the Metropolitan Police and the force with responsibility for policing the square mile of the city, the City of London Police, have large commercial investigation departments.

4.4   Typically, police involvement in financial investigations will be as a result of a referral from another agency; in the past this may have been the DTI and will certainly be the FSA in the future. When conducting investigations into alleged financial crime the police will commonly work in conjunction with other agencies and, in particular, the CPS. Until recently the CPS maintained a dedicated unit that would advise on serious fraud and related matters. Financial restrictions have now meant that local branches of the CPS are more likely to advise the police on matters of complex fraud, and it remains to be seen whether this is beneficial or not.

4.5   Once a matter is referred to the police it will investigate as the lead agency or in a supporting capacity. In respect of some procedural issues, the presence of the police is a statutory requirement; eg when exercising a warrant to enter premises and seize materials. Clearly in this instance the role of the police may be passive. However, when an allegation is of a serious nature it may the police who are the principal agency for the collation of evidence and preparation of materials for trial.

4.6   Actions taken by the police are governed by the Police and Criminal Evidence Act 1984 ('PACE 1984'). This legislation contains a number of provisions that are aimed at protecting a suspect from any improper or over-zealous police questioning, and the fundamental rights of all suspects who are subject to a criminal investigation are captured by this Act. In addition, the implementation of the Human Rights Act 1998 now enshrines the provisions of the European Convention on Human Rights in the UK's legislative order, and the courts must take cognisance of the provisions when considering the actions of the police during the evidence gathering and procedural stages of an inquiry.

4.7   The relationship between the police and the FSA is currently untested and it is not clear at this stage whether it would be the police or the FSA who would assume responsibility for taking the lead role in an investigation that was of a regulatory and criminal nature. Serious and complex frauds are generally investigated by the SFO, but not exclusively, and matters not dealt with by the SFO are investigated by the police and prosecuted by the CPS. Under the provisions of the Criminal Justice Act 1987 ('CJA 1987') it is for the Director of the SFO to decide whether or not to accept a case for investigation and trial. It is most likely that the FSA will follow this model and also decide on those matters that it is prepared to investigate and prosecute.

4.8   Given the extensive powers of the FSA, which are over and above those granted to the SFO, it is probably better to be subject to the traditional rules of evidence and be investigated and prosecuted by the police and the CPS than either the SFO or the FSA. It is unlikely, however, that a suspect will have any choice in the matter. There are disadvantages also, and since the devolution of centralised serious fraud case handling, these may increase. Police officers in England and Wales have considerable autonomy, and if it is the view of an investigating officer that there is no case to answer then a suspect may be released and the matter closed. Investigations into serious crimes will normally be conducted with the knowledge of the CPS and it may be asked for input and specialist advice at an early stage. Given that CPS case handling is now localised, like the police forces it advises, there is no central prosecution policy, and a suspect may find he is prosecuted in one part of the country for an offence that is not proceeded against in another area. This, of course, should not occur in cases where the matter is referred by the FSA.

4.9   The provisions of the PACE 1984 require the police to ensure that suspects are treated appropriately whilst in police custody, that all suspects have the opportunity to consult with a lawyer and that any questioning is conducted in accordance with agreed guidelines. Cases referred to the police by the FSA are likely to be charges which amount to serious frauds and money laundering – that is arrestable offences. It is the nature of criminal investigations that suspects are not always arrested at the earliest opportunity, and in respect of complex financial crimes the police will frequently have prepared questions that they are seeking to put to a suspect before he is brought into detention. On this basis a suspect may of course attend a police station voluntarily without having been arrested. If, during the course of such questioning, it becomes apparent that a criminal offence has been committed then the police are obliged to notify the suspect of their suspicions and caution him. Much has been said about the abolition of the right to silence and the introduction of the Criminal Justice and Public Order Act 1994, under which inferences can be drawn from a suspect's silence; however, the police do not have the power to compel a reluctant witness, or suspect, to answer questions.

4.10   During the course of a police investigation evidence may be gathered under the provisions of the Financial Services and Markets Act 2000 ('FSMA 2000') or established principles under the PACE 1984. Typically there will be a wide range of materials that have been obtained in a variety of formats. It is a well established principle of English law that material will not automatically be excluded from trial purely because the manner in which the evidence was obtained was itself illegal, for example taken by the police after an illegal search of premises. The FSMA 2000 builds upon the existing provisions for the obtaining of evidence and it may transpire that it supersedes some existing legislation, eg Bankers Book Evidence.

4.11   Neither police investigations conducted under the PACE 1984 nor any joint operations involving FSA and police under the FSMA 2000 can abrogate the sanctity of correspondence between lawyers and clients that is subject to 'legal privilege'. The meaning of this term is defined under the PACE 1984, s 10 as communications between a professional legal advisor and his client or any person representing his client made in connection with the giving of legal advice to the client. Protection is lost if any of the parties subject to the privilege intend that the documents should be used to further a criminal purpose. The appropriate channel to resolve disputes over the status of documents attracting legal privilege is judicial review.

4.12 The police have considerable powers of arrest and search without warrant. These powers are principally exercisable in respect of the previously mentioned arrestable offences. That is, criminal offences that can attract a term of imprisonment of five years or more on first conviction. Under s 18 of the PACE 1984 a police officer may enter and search any premises occupied or controlled by a person who is under arrest for an arrestable offence, if he has reasonable grounds for suspecting that there is on the premises evidence that relates to that offence, or some other arrestable offence which is connected with or similar to that offence. Any items found may be seized and retained. This wide power is extended further under s 19 of the PACE 1984 where once on the premises an officer may seize any item that he believes is evidence in relation to *any offence*. This includes any material held on computer, and he may demand that the information is produced in a form which can be taken away.

The Serious Fraud Office

4.13 It will be interesting to see how the relationship between the FSA and the SFO develops. In principle, the remit of the SFO is significantly narrower than that of the FSA and, accordingly, the potential for overlap between agency interests is slight. However, s 6 of the FSMA 2000 places a responsibility on the FSA to prevent and detect financial crimes, and fraud is specifically mentioned.

4.14 The SFO came into existence in April 1998. The legislative authority and powers of operation are located in the CJA 1987. The SFO exists to investigate and prosecute any suspected offence which appears, on reasonable grounds, to involve serious or complex fraud. It must be stated immediately that the creation of the SFO represented a turning point in English law as up until that time no agency had ever had authority to investigate and prosecute. Unlike the inquisitorial system in France, where an investigating magistrate has powers to conduct investigations and then propose disposal, in England the adversarial model has always sought to keep investigator and prosecutor as separate entities. Since the formation of the SFO the abrogation of investigatory and prosecutorial independence has been repeated by the creation of the FSA.

4.15   The SFO is staffed by permanent teams of lawyers and accountants, and these are supplemented by police officers on secondment from their own force. Fraud is not defined under English law and one might therefore be permitted to question what is it that the SFO investigates. However, the term 'serious fraud' is employed to limit the type of case to be investigated; in other words if the SFO do not wish to take over an investigation it will be returned to the police. This has worked fairly well so far, but of course the police are not of sufficient stature or legal independence perhaps to actually refuse to accept an SFO investigation. Whether the FSA will adopt such a view remains to be seen, though the authors of this book suspect it will not and that there will be considerable wrangling over ownership of cases.

4.16   The SFO has the power to demand that persons attend its offices and produce materials. Failure to do so is a criminal offence and attracts a custodial sanction. In this respect it is clear that the model for FSA powers has been the CJA 1987 and not the police powers under the PACE 1984. If the SFO decides to investigate a matter that does not fall within the scope of the term 'serious or complex fraud', this decision would be challengeable by way of judicial review.

4.17   We have seen previously that other agencies can join the FSA in conducting investigations. The SFO has a similar power to invite the police to join it, and the practical manifestation of this is that officers work at the SFO on detachment. These officers remain police officers throughout this period of time and they remain answerable to their respective Chief Officer of police; importantly the police officers are required to adhere to the provisions of the PACE 1984 whereas the lawyers and accountants are under no such obligation.

4.18   The FSA has committed itself to compliance with the Code for Crown Prosecutors. This is highly relevant when deciding on the appropriate disposal of a case. However, the FSA is not governed by the PACE 1984 and does not have police officers attached to it. Equally, there is no requirement on the SFO to utilise the services of the police, other than when executing a warrant; this is the position for the FSA. It will be interesting to see whether there is a development of police powers under SFO and FSA legislation to allow the police greater scope for involvement in serious fraud-type investigations, or whether in fact both agencies will seek to preserve their own identities and unique powers to differentiate between investigations conducted by professionals and those conducted by the police.

4.19   The scope of SFO powers has been subject to considerable discussion over the past 12 years, and the following points are worth consideration. Documents produced on demand may be copied, extracts taken and explanations about them must given. Failure to do so attracts a custodial penalty. If documents are not produced then the person required to produce them must state where they are; failure to do so attracts a custodial penalty. Both of these issues are of considerable significance as, unlike police investigations, the SFO can continue to investigate a matter after charge. The SFO has power to serve notice demanding production of documents or attendance of a person at a time and place specified by the SFO. There is no entitlement to any advance disclosure before complying with the notice and a notice may be served without any attempt to secure the documents or attendance informally. This, of course, was the main complaint against the SFO by Asil Nadir and Elizabeth Forsyth in the *Polly Peck* investigation as they claimed that had the SFO given informal advance notice then the collapse of the share price would not have occurred as swiftly as it did, ie over a period of a few hours once the City was aware that a warrant had been executed on the premises at South Audley Street.

4.20   There is an offence of falsifying, concealing, destroying or otherwise disposing of documents which an individual knows or suspects are relevant to a police or SFO investigation. Note the sentence is up to seven years' imprisonment and/or an unlimited fine on indictment, or up to six months' imprisonment and/or a fine up to the statutory maximum on summary conviction (CJA 1987, s 2(16)). There is no reason to think that the agency involvement would not extend to the FSA for the purposes of this section, particularly since a future role for the FSA in serious fraud investigations may be one similar to that of the DTI, ie the FSA may carry out the preliminary inquiry, the results of which are passed to the SFO.

Department of Trade and Industry investigations

4.21   It can be argued that many of the powers previously vested in the DTI have now been transferred to the FSA. Certainly this is true in respect of authority to investigate insider dealing and market manipulation and investigations into suspected fraud and irregular share dealing. However, the legislation that gives the Secretary of State the power to appoint investigators has not been repealed and both systems remain in place.

4.22   Under the Companies Act 1985 ('CA 1985') the DTI may investigate suspected frauds, alleged company malpractice and insider dealing. Rarely have any DTI investigations resulted in criminal prosecutions as normally the criminal investigations are conducted by the SFO on receipt of information from the DTI, e.g. *Guinness*[1] and *County NatWest*[2].

1   [1986] BCCC 43; affd [1998] 2 All ER 940, CA; on appeal [1990] 2 AC 663, HL.
2   [1999] Lloyd's Rep Bank 408, CA.

4.23   Under the CA 1985, s 447 the Secretary of State may, at any time, give directions to a company to produce specified documents. An explanation as to the contents or whereabouts of documents is mandatory, and failure to comply with any of the requirements is a criminal offence punishable with a fine. Section 447 inquiries are considered to be expeditious and are frequently utilised to establish whether there is a need for a further and more public investigation. The results of a s 447 investigation are not published and are largely private as the Secretary of State is under no obligation to report the findings to other bodies such as a Select Committee.

4.24   Under the CA 1985, s 432 inspectors can be appointed by the Secretary of State if a court declares that the affairs of the company should be investigated. These, and the rarely used s 431 powers, are exercised on application by a company or by its members. Such an order will be made where it is believed that the company's affairs have been conducted with intent to commit a fraud. The appointment of the s 432 inspectors is always made public. The aim of the investigation is to ascertain whether or not there have been irregularities in the managing of the company's affairs that constitute a winding up of the company or prosecutions being brought for criminal conduct. An investigator appointed under s 432 has considerable powers, including the power to enter premises by warrant and search for and seize materials, and to require production of documents and require any person to attend before him and answer questions. 'Any person' has a wide interpretation, including an officer or agent of the company; this means past as well as present officers or agents, and agents includes 'bankers and solicitors and persons employed by it as auditors, whether or not these persons are or are not officers of the company or other body corporate' (CA 1985, s 434(4)). Challenge to the exercise of the functions of an appointed investigator is through judicial review.

4.25   Documents may be obtained without notice. A magistrate may issue a warrant on application which is exercisable by a police officer, who may of course be accompanied by a named person. Since the warrant is issued to the police and not the DTI, the provisions of the PACE 1984 will apply. It is the responsibility of the police to control the events at the premises whilst a search is being conducted otherwise the search may be deemed to be unlawful. There is no power to search without a warrant and entry with a warrant is only permitted on one occasion.

4.26   Witnesses to DTI investigations are frequently asked to attend an informal interview which may lead to a formal interview at a later stage in time. The informal interview is not usually taped and attendance is optional. Failure to attend may of course result in a request to attend a formal interview which will be tape-recorded. The recording of interviews is not governed by the PACE 1984; however, inspectors will adhere to guidelines contained within the Investigation Handbook. The question of whether information obtained during a civil process can subsequently be used against a defendant at his criminal trial has been subject to considerable commentary and decisions at all levels in the English courts as well as in Strasbourg. Commentary on this area will be discussed in Chapter 5. What should be borne in mind is that there is a general requirement that DTI inspectors should act fairly at all times, and the Investigation Handbook recommends that once inspectors have prepared the first draft of their report ' ... they may think it appropriate ... to write to the witness setting out the intended criticisms with notice of the evidence on which they are based, giving him a fixed period of, for example, twenty one days to respond'[1].

1   DTI Investigation Handbook, Appendix B, para 41.

4.27   Before leaving this area it should be remembered that the DTI do have authority to investigate suspected cases of insider dealing and market manipulation. However, as we have seen, there are considerable areas of duplication in respect of DTI and FSA powers and it can be anticipated that future insider dealing cases will, in the first instance, be investigated by the FSA.

Inland Revenue investigations

4.28   One of the principal objectives of the Inland Revenue is to identify and correct non-compliance. To achieve this it uses a range of measures including appropriate use of audit, enquiry and recovery powers. On average, 1 in 200 companies and 1 in 100 unincorporated businesses are subjected to a full investigation per annum. To effectively conduct investigations the Inland Revenue has created a number of specialist departments. These include the Special Investigations Section, the Special Trade Investigations Unit, the International Division, Financial Intermediaries and Claims Office and the Large Business Office. The Large Business Office deals with reviewing the accounts of the largest UK corporate taxpayers such as the banks, building societies, insurance companies, Lloyds of London and the Stock Exchange. The high level of expertise and technical resource within the Large Business Office should not be underestimated, and the ratio between enforcement costs activity and tax paid as a direct result of that activity was 57:1 for the year ending 1999. The actual tax yield for the period was £1886 million[1].

1   Inland Revenue Annual Report 1999.

4.29   In cases of tax fraud the Inland Revenue may accept a money settlement or the Board of Inland Revenue may institute criminal proceedings. The problem that this creates for a suspect is that it may not be clear which option the Inland Revenue is exercising until some way into an inquiry. Either way, the principal source of authority is the Taxes Management Act 1970. Investigations are conducted under the provisions of a Code of Practice, and subsequent prosecutions will be brought by dedicated prosecution groups of which there are currently four within the Special Compliance Office.

4.30 The policy on prosecutions was stated in the Keith Committee Report in 1983 as: 'In the main the department deals with the tax evader not by prosecution but by money penalties graded according to the gravity of the offence'[1]. Little has changed, and there are very few criminal prosecutions other than where there is evidence of serious fraud. On this basis the likelihood of a criminal prosecution can be reduced down to where there is deception, conspiracy, corruption, organised fraud, unusual fraud or repeated phoenixism and money laundering.

1 The Committee on Enforcement Powers of the Revenue Departments, Cmnd 8822, para 9.10.

4.31 In common with a number of powers previously discussed, the financial services suspect is subject to investigative provisions that are exceptional and unique. In this instance this does not extend to compelling a suspect to attend offices and make disclosures. However, the Hansard practice, of allowing suspects to make a full disclosure in return for consideration of non-prosecution, does not mean that what has been said during an interview will be subsequently inadmissible during a criminal prosecution (Taxes Management Act 1970, s 105). In light of the Human Rights Act 1998 there may be suitable grounds to challenge the provisions of s 105.

4.32 The Inland Revenue are given statutory authority to make disclosures to the FSA under the FSMA 2000, s 350, whereby 'No obligation as to secrecy imposed by statute or otherwise prevents the disclosure of Revenue information to the Authority or Secretary of State'. There are restrictions on the use of this information, but all the criminal offences under the FSMA 2000 are exceptions to the restrictions (FSMA 2000, s 350(4)(c)).

4.33 Under the Taxes Management Act 1970, s 20 the Inland Revenue can demand the production of documents, and this can extend to a notice of requirement being served on a third party. The powers are not as wide as the CJA 1987 or the FSMA 2000 powers, however, as production of materials is restricted to 'such documents as are in his possession or power and contain, or may contain, information relevant to any tax liability to which the taxpayer is or may be, or may have been, subject to' (Taxes Management Act 1970, s 20(3)). The documents requested must be specified; the legislation does not permit fishing trips.

4.34 Any person who falsifies, conceals, destroys or otherwise disposes of a document subject to a s 20 notice, or permits another person to do so, is liable to a custodial sentence of up to two years' imprisonment and/or an unlimited fine on indictment, or six months' imprisonment and a fine up to the statutory maximum on summary conviction. You do not have to wait until being served with a notice to supply documents to commit the offence; ie if you destroy a document in anticipation of being requested to supply it the offence is complete at the time that you destroyed it.

4.35   Inland Revenue officers may apply to a circuit judge for a warrant to enter and search premises. Entry may be by force if necessary and a warrant must be executed within 14 days of being granted. Applications for issuing a warrant are ex parte and the owner of the premises has no right to be heard. It is not necessary for a police officer to accompany Inland Revenue officers when they execute a warrant, albeit in practice an officer in uniform will normally be present.

It should be noted that if a warrant is executed at the premises of a legal advisor then he is not obliged to hand over any document that might attract professional privilege, unless the client gives his consent. For the purposes of tax matters, professional privilege means legal advice, correspondence between client and legal advisor in which legal advice is given, and documents created for the purposes of instructing counsel.

4.36   Under the provisions of the Finance Act 2000 the Inland Revenue may now demand the production of documents, such as those that are obtainable and held by a solicitor, without the need to execute a search warrant. What the new provisions seem to be aimed at is providing a route by which the Inland Revenue can secure the release of documents from a legal advisor where the advisor is not the subject of the investigation and a demand to produce documents is less disruptive than a search being conducted at working premises.

4.37   An additional tax-related offence is introduced under the Finance Act 2000, s 144 where it now becomes an offence to knowingly be concerned in the fraudulent evasion of tax by oneself or any other person. This offence attracts up to seven years' imprisonment and/or an unlimited fine on indictment and up to six months and/or a fine up to the statutory maximum when heard at the magistrate's court.

4.38   Should an inquiry reveal criminal offences and a suspect be arrested then Inland Revenue officers will question in accordance with the provisions of the PACE 1984 and adhere to the relevant PACE 1984 Codes of Practice.

4.39   Tax evasion and money laundering are frequently connected issues and facilitating another to retain the profits of any criminal conduct is an offence. This is the case irrespective of whether assistance is given onshore, offshore or in the virtual environment, as the associated conduct (ie tax evasion) is invariably a criminal offence under all tangible and intangible jurisdictions. Tax practitioners are subject to all of the money laundering provisions, and any future manifestations of inter-agency co-operation are most likely to be apparent in this sphere of criminal enterprise.

Director General of Fair Trading investigations

4.40   The role of the Office of Fair Trading has altered considerably in the past year, partially as a result of the implementation of the FSMA 2000, and more specifically as a result of the Competition Act 1998, which came into force on 1 March 2000. Whilst it is not within the scope of this work to discuss in detail the provisions of the Competition Act 1998 it should be borne in mind that the Act has completely re-shaped UK competition law by virtually rendering the Restrictive Trade Practices Act 1976 obsolete and introducing a model of competition law that is now clearly compliant with European competition law and conduct. At first glance it may appear that in future any agreement that seeks to grant exclusivity, fix prices or guarantee market dominance may be investigated under Competition Act powers and the FSMA 2000. But the provisions are not quite this wide and there are a number of restrictions.

4.41   There are two principal areas where the interface between the FSA and DGFT is likely to be most prominent. One is in relation to consumer credit, and there are apparently options available to the DGFT as to whether powers of intervention are exercised under the FSMA 2000 or the Consumer Credit Act 1974. The types of consumer credit-related offending that will attract joint agency interest are offences involving fraud or discrimination or business practices based on oppressive or deceitful behaviour.

4.42   The second area is competition. In respect of competition within the financial services environment, a separate regime has been created. Under the FSMA 2000, ss 311 and 312 there is a general exclusion from the provisions of the Competition Act 1998 for recognised investment exchanges, clearing houses and specified other bodies.

4.43   The apparent lacuna created by this provision is not insurmountable for the purposes of effective regulation, as the FSA is required to inform the DGFT of all the regulatory provisions and other relevant information it receives in support of an application for recognition. It is then incumbent upon the DGFT to make a report as to whether any of the provisions are likely to have an adverse effect on competition (FSMA 2000, ss 303 and 304). In order to evaluate the position fully the DGFT needs statutory authority to gather relevant information.

4.44   Under the FSMA 2000, s 305 the DGFT has the power to conduct investigations and request that documents are produced. In addition he may demand the supply of information from any person. Failure to comply with a request is an offence and will be treated as a contempt of court. Misleading or supplying false information to the DGFT is a criminal offence.

4.45   The deliberate overlap of the Competition Act 1998 and the FSMA 2000 functions is specifically referred to under s 399 of the FSMA 2000 where, in relation to offences involving the provision of false or misleading information, s 44 of the Competition Act 1998 applies in relation to any function of the DGFT as if it were a function under Part I of that Act.

4.46   Information about individuals or companies obtained by the DGFT may not generally be disclosed. Where the information relates to an individual, it may not be disclosed during that individual's lifetime; if it relates to a company then the relevant period is whilst business is still being conducted. However, under the FSMA 2000, s 351(2) disclosure may be made if it is for the purposes of assisting in criminal proceedings or the investigation of any criminal offence.

4.47   Whereas the FSMA 2000 statutorily excludes certain financial providers from the new Competition Act, the general emphasis on preventing financial crimes under the FSMA 2000 means that investigations conducted by the DGFT may well stimulate FSA involvement indirectly. It is therefore worth concluding this section by making reference to the provisions of the new Competition Act and familiarising oneself with the broad range of powers vested in the DGFT. The Competition Act 1998 gives the DGFT powers to require documents or specific information (s 26), enter premises without a warrant (s 27) and enter and search premises with a warrant (s 27). The basis for exercising any of these powers is that the DGFT has reasonable grounds for suspecting an offence. Ascertaining a reasonable ground for suspicion would typically come from information supplied by an employee or ex-employee, meetings with the Office of Fair Trading or informal enquiries.

4.48   Any demands for information must be specific and state the subject matter sought as well as a precise description of the documents or categories of documents requested. In addition, the DGFT must set out the nature of the offences that have allegedly been committed.

4.49   Investigations may be conducted without a warrant, and an appointed DGFT investigator may enter any premises (this extends to domestic premises if they are used for business purposes or if business documents are kept there) and take copies or extracts of any materials he considers relevant to that investigation. The DGFT has stated that non-warrant visits will normally be conducted during office hours.

4.50   On application to a High Court judge the DGFT may apply for a warrant to enter any premises, by force if necessary, if the DGFT has previously requested documents which have not been produced and it is reasonably believed that they are on the stated premises. Warrants of this nature must be executed within one month of issue. A person can refuse to disclose a document that is privileged information. The provisions of the *Saunders*[1] ruling and the Human Rights Act 1998 will apply in respect of self-incriminatory disclosures. This does not preclude the DGFT from making disclosures to the FSA under the FSMA 2000.

1   (1996) 23 EHRR 313, [1998] 1 BCLC 362.

4.51 There are a number of criminal offences contained within the Competition Act 1998. Investigations into such matters will then typically invoke the provisions of the FSMA 2000 relating to disclosure of material where an investigation into *any* criminal offence is being conducted.

4.52 The Competition Act 1998 criminal offences are:

- failing to comply with a production requirement (unlimited fine on indictment, up to statutory maximum on summary conviction);
- intentionally obstructing an investigator *without* a warrant (unlimited fine on indictment, up to statutory maximum on summary conviction);
- intentionally obstructing an investigator *with* a warrant (up to two years' imprisonment and/or an unlimited fine on indictment, up to statutory maximum on summary conviction);
- intentionally or recklessly destroying, concealing, falsifying or causing or permitting a document to be destroyed, concealed or falsified (up to two years' imprisonment and/or unlimited fine, up to statutory maximum on summary conviction); and
- knowingly or recklessly providing false or misleading information (up to two years' imprisonment and/or unlimited fine on indictment, up to statutory maximum on summary conviction).

4.53 The DGFT may also impose fines of up to 10% of turnover in the UK in respect of infringements that are contrary to the provisions contained within Chapters 1 and 2 of the Competition Act 1998. It is worth noting that the criminal understanding of terms such as 'intentionally' and 'recklessly' are not applicable, and infringements may be committed intentionally or negligently and ignorance or mistakes will not prevent a finding of guilt.

4.54 It is clear from the wording in the FSMA 2000 that there is a distinction between general DGFT provisions and financial services. Nevertheless, the new regime does significantly alter the face of competition law and there is likely to be some overlap between the areas of interests that are outside of the FSMA 2000 and within. For a comprehensive overview of the new Competition Act see 'The Competition Act – A Guide' at www.tarlolyons.co. The powers and the Act can be accessed through the Office of Fair Trading website at www.oft.gov.uk.

Customs and Excise

4.55 Customs duties apply to goods that move across a country's borders; excise duty applies to the movement of goods within a country's own borders. Since becoming members of the European Union the rules that govern our customs duties are subject to European Directives. Due to the complexity of the rules and the reduction of border controls within the European member states, the opportunity for criminals to commit large-scale transnational frauds has increased substantially.

4.56 There are a number of criminal offences that may be investigated by Customs, and subsequent proceedings will be instituted by Customs and Excise or the CPS. In this section there will be a brief overview of the principal excise and customs offences as well as a discussion of the potential areas for inter-agency investigations.

4.57 Under the Value Added Tax Act 1994 it is an offence to evade, or intend to evade, liability or to falsely claim credit. Maximum penalties are seven years' imprisonment and/or an unlimited fine on indictment, or up to six months' imprisonment and/or a fine up to the statutory maximum. There are also related offences of intentionally making a false statement or furnishing false details. In common with the powers of the FSA, it is possible to proceed via civil sanctions rather than criminal trial. Whether the imposition of a fine under these circumstances amounts to a penal sanction for the purposes of the Human Rights Act 1998 will be discussed in Chapter 5; case law from the European Court of Human Rights in the seminal decision of *Funke v France*[1] would absolutely confirm the answer as positive: the sanctions are criminal.

1   [1993] 1 CMLR 897, 16 EHRR 297, ECtHR.

4.58 Under the Value Added Tax Act 1994, s 72 it is an offence to take, or assist another in taking, steps to fraudulently evade duty. This offence attracts a potential seven years custodial sentence and/or an unlimited fine on indictment, or six months and/or a fine up to the statutory maximum at summary trial. Under the Customs and Excise Management Act 1979 there are a range of offences specifically designed to deal with evasion of duty liability. These offences include knowingly or recklessly making untrue declarations, counterfeiting documents and money laundering.

4.59 In order that investigations may be conducted, customs officers have the power to enter premises without a warrant and search for and seize evidence. In addition, a magistrate may issue a warrant to permit entry to any premises, by force if necessary, on receipt of evidence to the effect that there are reasonable grounds to believe that a serious VAT fraud is being committed on the premises. Interestingly, and somewhat uniquely, this warrant will also permit customs officers to search any person found on those premises. Section 10(3)(c) of the Value Added Tax Act 1994 states that ' ... no woman or girl shall be searched except by a woman'. The legislation does not stipulate that men must be searched by male customs officers only.

4.60 Cheating the public revenue is an offence at common law and will include any fraudulent act that diverts money from the Inland Revenue. Conspiracy to defraud was a common law offence but has now been repealed by s 12 of the CJA 1987. A person guilty of conspiracy to defraud is liable on conviction on indictment to a term of imprisonment not exceeding ten years and/or an unlimited fine. It is of note that the jurisdiction of the offence of conspiracy to defraud has now been extended under Part 1 of the Criminal Justice Act 1993 ('CJA 1993'), which was finally introduced during the latter part of 2000. A conspiracy to defraud may now be committed outside of England and Wales and, in addition, anyone who assists or induces another to conspire to defraud another EU state may be prosecuted in the UK.

4.61   A number of the principal customs offences are legislated against under the CJA 1993. Section 71 of this Act makes it an offence for a person who, in the UK, assists or induces any conduct outside the UK which involves the commission of a serious offence against the law of another member state. The offences referred to in the CJA 1993 include evading Community duty or tax and obtaining refunds and repayments, relief or exemptions. But this list is not exhaustive and, in essence, any serious criminal offence is captured by the provisions. The crucial element for prosecuting authorities is to prove that the matter charged does amount to a 'serious criminal offence' in the relevant other EU state.

4.62   Under the Customs and Excise Management Act 1979 there are powers to examine goods at a time and place specified by the Commissioner (s 159), take samples of goods inspected (s 160), apply for a magistrate's warrant to enter any premises, by force if necessary (s 160(3)), and search vehicles and vessels (s 163). Customs officers also have the power to stop any person arriving or leaving the UK and search that person (s 164). Also, the majority of offences outlined above are punishable with a custodial sentence in excess of five years and therefore they are arrestable offences. As we have seen previously, under the provisions of the PACE 1984, upon arrest for an arrestable offence the premises or vehicle where a person is at the time of arrest may be searched without warrant. Investigations by customs officers are subject to the provisions of the PACE 1984 as they are deemed to be persons 'other than police officers who are charged with the duty of investigating offences and charging offenders' (PACE 1994, s 67(9)).

4.63   Although a power of arrest is attached to most of the offences that customs officers may investigate, they do not have the authority to charge a person with an offence, release them or bail or remand them in police custody pending appearance before a magistrate. Common practice is for customs officers to interview suspects and then present them before a police custody officer; he will then decide on the appropriate discharge of the matter.

Investigations in the context of insolvency

4.64   It is not surprising that a number of investigations into the business operations of a company commence when it has encountered substantial trading or financial difficulties. If a receiver has been appointed under the terms of a debenture or if the company has gone into liquidation, the activities of the company are considered objectively from a very different perspective. Indeed, it is not an infrequent occurrence that matters are discovered by the insolvency practitioners which in turn lead to an investigation by regulatory authorities into the activities of the company, its directors and employees. There is a duty on insolvency practitioners to report any apparent contraventions of the general prohibition to the FSA without delay (FSMA 2000, ss 364 and 370).

4.65 In any case, where there has been a winding-up order made by a court (for example, because a company is unable to pay its debts), the Official Receiver is under an obligation to investigate the causes of the company's failure. The Official Receiver also has to investigate in any case the promotion, formation, business dealings and affairs of the company. Such investigations have led in due course to proceedings being brought against directors and others. These include proceedings for the recovery of the company's property, and the consequences of wrongful trading, and granting preferences or entering into transactions at an undervalue. The report which is produced by the Official Receiver is, in any case, an important document for the purpose of any subsequent proceedings, and indeed is evidence of the facts stated within it. This applies to proceedings under the Company Directors Disqualification Act 1986, if such proceedings are commenced after the Secretary of State has considered the Official Receiver's report.

4.66 The Official Receiver (or liquidator) has a wide range of powers (if he needs them) to enable him to carry out his inquiries into the management and affairs of the company with the maximum amount of information. Under the Insolvency Act, 1986 ('IA 1986'), s 236 an application can be made to the court for an order summoning an officer of the company, or particular persons who have relevant information regarding the promotion, formation, business, dealings or affairs or property of the company. In addition, persons suspected of having company property in their possession, or those who are indebted to the company, may be summoned. There are statutory obligations to co-operate with the Official Receiver. The court can order a private examination under oath and has powers to order the delivery up of company property or the payment of any sum due by way of debt to the company.

The court may also order the swearing of an affidavit setting out the deponent's dealings with the company, and require the production of books, papers or other records.

4.67 When an application is made to the court for an order for the examination of witnesses, the court exercises a discretion whether or not to make the order. The courts are of course concerned that such wide-ranging powers should not be used as an instrument of oppression. Relevant principles when considering whether to make an order include the following:

- the order should not be made if it has the effect of putting the company in a better position than it would have been in if there had been no liquidation;
- all that has to be shown is that there is a reasonable requirement for the particular information sought;
- the court is more sympathetic to making an order in respect of former officers of the company to give evidence rather than persons not in that category; and
- the court is more inclined to make an order in respect of the provision of documents as opposed to examination under oath.

4.68   One of the practical problems which has arisen is that the party against whom an order is sought under the IA 1986, s 236 may (or his employer or principal may) be a possible defendant to proceedings brought by the liquidator, for example for negligence. In those circumstances it may well be oppressive to allow cross-examination of the third party when the main point of the exercise is not to locate assets but to obtain evidence for use in such potential proceedings.

4.69   Assuming that a court has made an order under the IA 1986, s 236 for the examination of a person under oath, can they then refuse to answer any questions on the grounds that they may incriminate themselves? The short answer is 'no' (see *Bishopsgate Investment Management Ltd v Maxwell*[1]). The whole point of the section is that there is a class of persons who have information which may be of assistance to the liquidator. It would defeat the purpose of obtaining such information or other assistance if the proposed examinee could decline to answer if those answers might incriminate him. Under the IA 1986, s 433 any such answers are admissible in civil or criminal proceedings. However, particularly in view of *Saunders v United Kingdom*[2], it seems unlikely that reliance would normally be placed on any such answers given or information supplied in the criminal courts.

1   [1993] Ch 1, [1992] 2 All ER 856, CA.
2   (1996) 23 EHRR 313, [1998] 1 BCLC 362.

4.70   Ernest Saunders was obliged to answer questions posed by DTI inspectors enquiring into the Guinness unlawful share support operation. He was subject to proceedings for contempt of court if he refused. The criminal trial judge admitted the answers given under compulsion which the prosecution relied upon to prove his involvement in the operation and to prove what was said to be his dishonesty. The European Court of Human Rights held that on the facts there had been an infringement of Mr Saunders' right not to incriminate himself, a right afforded by art 6 of the European Convention on Human Rights.

4.71   In future cases, while the power of the court to order an examination under the IA 1986, s 236 remains as before, the use to which any answers will be put, particularly in criminal proceedings, will be carefully scrutinised. Under the PACE 1984, s 78 the trial judge has a discretion to exclude evidence. It is highly probable that any such evidence would be excluded if the judge decided that any admission in evidence of answers given under compulsion undermined the fairness of the proceedings. Similar issues are faced when the SFO exercises its powers under the CJA 1987, s 2, albeit that any answers obtained under compulsion are not admissible unless the deponent gives evidence: see *Re Arrows (No 4)*[1].

1   [1994] 3 All ER 814.

4.72   Confidentiality is another factor which has to be considered. This particularly arises when an office holder promises confidentiality to a person from whom he is seeking information. He is entitled to that information under the IA 1986, s 235, and he may offer some form of confidentiality so that he does not have to obtain a court order under the IA 1986, s 236. In principle, if there is a criminal trial and the prosecution or defence wish to examine the transcripts of the interviews, they are not entitled as of right to do so. However, the criminal trial judge may come to the conclusion that in order to secure a fair trial it is necessary to issue a summons in order to require the production of the transcripts.

4.73   If a court does make an order under the IA 1986, s 236, then it can impose conditions on the availability of the transcripts, although these complex provisions have given rise to a number of difficulties. There have been a number of reported cases dealing with the inter-play of various statutory provisions. Of most importance in terms of outcome is the undoubted ability of the SFO to seek compulsorily copies of transcripts obtained by a liquidator under the IA 1986, s 236. Other cases demonstrate problems which arise when the Companies Court is asked to make orders under the IA 1986, s 236 and attempts are made to impose restrictions upon the use to which they may be put by investigative bodies. It is also possible for liquidators to obtain orders for DTI inspectors to disclose to the liquidators information obtained by the inspectors under compulsion. It will be apparent from the above broad summary that there are extensive powers enabling many bodies not only to obtain information by compulsion but also to request copies of documents obtained by others under compulsion.

4.74   A frequent occurrence is for a liquidator to use his powers under the IA 1986, s 235 in order to obtain by private examination information about a company's affairs and dealings, and to trace any of its assets to which he lays claim. The latter can give rise to complex claims, but it is obvious that by using these extensive powers swiftly, the ability of the liquidator to locate and, if possible, recover any assets which have been disposed of is considerably enhanced. It is, of course, advisable to co-operate fully with any such investigation.

Disciplinary and in-house

4.75   Another way in which investigations are initiated is when there is an internal enquiry. Sometimes these are driven by some form of action which may give rise to disciplinary proceedings. This section describes the issues which can arise in an employment context, the way in which such an enquiry may function, and the Regulation of Investigatory Powers Act 2000.

4.76   Obviously, any employer may decide to hold an enquiry into particular events, and any employee would be expected to assist in any such enquiry. Although a contract of employment may be expected to contain detailed provisions regarding both parties' obligations, there are (subject to those express terms) frequently duties implied as a matter of law. Some of those implied terms are dealt with in outline here, but it must be appreciated that such implied terms will yield to the express terms contained in a contract of employment.

4.77   The implied terms include the following: under the terms of an employee's contract of employment, an employee holding himself out to have particular skills to do a particular type of work, and who is employed on that basis, by implication undertakes that he possesses and will exercise reasonable skill or competence in performing his duties. In addition, an employee is usually subject to an implied term that he will exercise reasonable care in the performance of his duties. And an employee will be expected to obey the lawful and reasonable orders of his employer in so far as they are within the scope of that employee's employment that he agreed to undertake.

4.78   The other duty, which may of occasion be described as a flexible duty, is that of fidelity. Obviously, any employee is expected to serve his employer with honesty and with good faith, and this is another term which is frequently implied (subject to any express terms) as a matter of law. It is this duty which prevents an employee (again most modern contracts will provide expressly for such an eventuality) from approaching or dealing with his employer's clients during the course of his employment other than for the account of his employer. Absent any such express terms (which there will almost invariably be in a relevant contract of sophistication) there may be no limitations upon what an employee is able to do after the termination of his employment.

4.79   Another term which is frequently an express term, but which in the absence of such a term is implied by law, is the obligation not to disclose confidential information. There can of course be argument as to whether a particular type of information constitutes confidential information for these purposes. In addition, there is an implied term preventing an employee from making use of any confidential information to the detriment of the employer. In the absence of any express terms (or indeed sometimes when there is such a term) the classification of information into what is properly 'confidential' can sometimes be difficult. This is partly because of the difficulty of drafting such a clause, and partly because an employee is entitled to build up his own store of knowledge and experience in so far as it is honestly acquired during the course of his employment. Once a contract of employment has ended, the usual rule is that it is only trade secrets which can be protected from disclosure. One of the reasons for this is that employers have in the past used such terms as reasons for preventing ex-employees from competing with them upon termination of their employment. There are exceptions to such obligations not to make disclosure under the 'whistle-blowing' provisions of the Public Interest Disclosure Act 1998.

4.80   Another important implied term is the duty on the part of an employer not to undermine his employee's trust and confidence. This term has been extended by the courts in a number of decisions. For example, the BCCI affair gave rise to a number of employees claiming stigma damages based upon the activities of their employer and their inability to obtain other work.

4.81   The context of any enquiry conducted by an employer may well have both a disciplinary and a fact-finding aspect. If events have occurred leading to a possible claim against the employer (or indeed by the employer) then there may be an overlapping need to consider whether there has been a breach of contract by one or more employees. Sometimes such an enquiry will be conducted by external lawyers or accountants. Sometimes it will be conducted purely on an in-house basis. Clearly the precise form of that enquiry will depend on a number of different factors. These would include the nature and scale of the act or omission which is the subject of the enquiry; the nature and scale of the consequences of that act or omission; the persons conducting it; and the likely consequences or ramifications of such an enquiry.

4.82   In the context of unfair dismissal, subject to a qualification period most employees have a right not to be unfairly dismissed. If a person has been dismissed, then in order to assess whether a dismissal was fair or unfair, the first stage to consider is what was the reason or the principal reason for the dismissal. Once that reason or principal reason has been identified, and the burden is on the employer to show what it was, then such a reason has to be a substantial reason for the dismissal and has to fall within the list of substantial reasons given in the Employment Rights Act 1996. This list includes such matters as the conduct of the employee, his capability, or some other substantial reason of a kind which justifies the dismissal of an employee holding the position held by that employee.

4.83   At the second stage, the issue is whether the employer acted reasonably in treating the reason as a sufficient reason for dismissing the employee. Tribunals are concerned with both the procedural and substantive aspects when considering the question of reasonableness. As far as the substantive element is concerned, the tribunal will carry out a careful investigation into the background to the dismissal. It will also carry out a review of the procedural aspects of the dismissal. Was the dismissal sufficiently serious such that no warning was necessary, or should a warning have been given? Should some opportunity for improvement have been given? In addition, the manner of the investigation is considered. In large organisations, there is frequently an enquiry at which representation may be possible. Indeed, one of the factors taken into account by a tribunal in assessing reasonableness is the size of the employer and the administrative resources available to it. The enquiry affords the employee an opportunity to be heard, so that the reasons for dismissal can be considered by the employee and commented upon by him.

4.84   At the enquiry carried out by the employer, clearly only those facts and circumstances known to the employer at the time can be acted upon. Facts which later emerge may be relevant to the level of any compensation. All of the circumstances are reviewed by any tribunal, including the availablity of an appeal.

4.85   It will be apparent from the above that there will frequently be an enquiry when disciplinary matters are raised. It is frequently the case that recordings are made of telephone conversations and they will be considered if relevant, as will the contents of e-mails. Under the Regulation of Investigatory Powers Act 2000, it is an offence for a person intentionally and unlawfully to intercept within the UK any communication in the course of transmission by means of a public postal service or a public telecommunication system. A private telecommunication system is excluded from control provided the person carrying out the interception is the one who has a right to control the operation or use of the system or if he has the express or implied consent of such a person to make the interception. A telecommunication system covers any system which facilitates the transmission of communications by any means involving the use of electrical or electromagnetic energy. Regulations made under the Regulation of Investigatory Powers Act 2000 provide when any interception may be lawful. This includes the situation where the operator of a system monitors communications or keeps a record of communications in order to establish facts, or to ascertain compliance with regulatory or self-regulatory practices which are applicable to the system controller in the carrying on of his business, or to prevent or detect crime.

4.86   Under these provisions, an employer who has his own e-mail system will be able to monitor communications and to keep a record of any such communications which is relevant to the employer's business. This would include not only a communication dealing with a transaction made in the course of that business but also a communication which relates to that business.

Conclusion

4.87   The plethora of powers outlined above makes it abundantly clear that there are sufficient sanctions available to prevent and detect specific and generic financial services-related criminality. A number of the powers were introduced before the implementation of the Human Rights Act 1998; however, the UK was one of the first states to sign up to the concept of a European Convention on Human Rights and, almost ironically, the most challenged article, art 6, the right to a fair trial, is known as the 'English Article'.

4.88   The exercise of many of the powers above will now have to be undertaken with greater care and with consideration of the new Human Rights legislation. All of the agencies referred to are public bodies and it is incumbent upon them to ensure the protection of rights for individuals and bodies corporate. At all times the overriding question must be: is the action taken proportionate and necessary? In addition to art 6-type applications, the right to privacy, art 8, will feature increasingly in the future.

4.89   The financial service industry represents a considerable asset to the public and private economic wealth of the UK. The regulation of companies and individuals must be balanced against this with sanctions that are neither draconian nor ineffective. The implementation of the Human Rights Act 1998 will go some considerable way towards ensuring that appropriate levels of protection are enshrined and the financial sector can anticipate a new and fertile territory being explored by defence lawyers who are seeking to establish that companies have human rights also.

4.90   As we have seen, under the FSMA 2000, s 354 the FSA are statutorily obliged to co-operate with other UK, and overseas, regulators and enforcement agencies. It is required to share information with the Secretary of State and any other authority that has a responsibility for the regulation of financial services, and most others in the prevention and detection of financial crime: 'Co-operation may include the sharing of information which the Authority is not prevented from disclosing'. It would appear that the catch all provisions of s 6 of the FSMA 2000 are sufficiently wide to ensure that there will always be a power available to justify the actions of an investigation agency; whether this translates into compatibility with the Human Rights Act 1998 has yet to be tested before the courts. On this basis it will be most interesting to observe the degree of enthusiasm that the FSA displays for mounting inter-agency investigations and prosecutions.

CHAPTER 5

Evidence and enforcement

Introduction

5.1 This chapter addresses the key concepts of disclosure in both civil and criminal proceedings, although in each case there are different meanings attached to the term. As explained in more detail below, in civil proceedings there is an obligation to retain and to disclose a range of documents which relate to the issues between the parties. These are not just hard copy documents as, unsurprisingly, this extends to information stored electronically.

5.2 Criminal proceedings have their own rules relating to the obtaining, production and disclosure of documents. While the rules in civil proceedings have been substantially reformed, the rules in criminal cases have been criticised for being archaic and are currently being scrutinised with a view to making them more modern and appropriate for the 21st century.

5.3 Disclosure in the senses used in paras **5.1** and **5.2** is an important area and of immediate practical application. In order to understand the concepts of disclosure, some aspects of the law of evidence such as privilege and public interest immunity need to be outlined, and these are dealt with below.

5.4 The Financial Services and Markets Act 2000 ('FSMA 2000') itself contains provisions (dealt with in paras **2.16** and **2.42**) by which an investigator appointed by an investigating authority has power to require the production of specified documents or categories of documents which are relevant to the investigation. Here we will discuss the principles of disclosure in both the civil and the criminal fields.

5.5 Another related area of importance is freezing orders, formerly known as the 'Mareva injunction', the underlying principles of which will also be discussed. It is frequently the case that when such orders are made (often prior to the commencement of the proceedings themselves) freezing particular assets or assets generally, related orders are made providing for the production of documents by the defendant. One of the themes referred to below is the privilege against self-incrimination, and this is of importance in some cases where, by the making of an appropriate statement or by the production of particular documents, a party may provide evidence of an incriminating nature. This is another area where reform is being actively considered.

Civil proceedings

Civil procedure – the new code

5.6 On 26 April 1999, the new Civil Procedure Rules ('CPR') came into force. The old Rules relating to procedural matters in the civil courts were swept away and replaced by a brand new code. There is a new overriding objective which has to be applied whenever any rule is being interpreted or whenever the court is asked to make an order. This is the overriding objective of ensuring that cases are dealt with justly.

5.7 This objective is defined by ensuring, so far as is practicable, that the parties are on an equal footing, that expense is saved and that the case is dealt with in a way that is proportionate to the amount of money involved, to the importance of the case, to the complexity of the issues, and to the financial position of each party. The case must be dealt with expeditiously and fairly, and an appropriate share of the court's resources must be allotted to it, while taking into account the need to allot resources to other cases. As a further demonstration of a sea-change in approach, the parties are required to help the court to further the overriding objective.

Disclosure

5.8 One of the areas of change brought about by the new CPR was what used to be called 'discovery', now called 'disclosure'. This is the process whereby each side in civil litigation collates and makes available to the other parties in the litigation a list of the documents which it has or which it can provide. Facilities for inspecting those documents are made and copies can be taken. There are categories of documents excluded from such a process, for example those which attract legal professional privilege.

5.9 The old discovery process came in for a lot of criticism. The parties set out their case in what used to be called 'pleadings', now called 'the statement of case'. From those documents the issues in play could be identified. Each of the parties then had to list all of the documents in its possession, custody or power that were relevant to those issues. One of the problems which gave rise to practical difficulties and also escalated the range (and cost) of the discovery exercise was the test for relevance of a particular document. The test extended beyond any document which may advance one's own case and a document which might damage another's case; it also included any documents which may fairly lead to a train of enquiry which might have either of those two consequences.

5.10 In cases of any complexity, the burden of providing discovery was extensive, particularly since a large number of documents disclosed, while 'relevant' under the extended test, in reality had nothing to do with the case at all. Discovery could, particularly in view of the time taken searching for documents and the legal costs involved, become an oppressive exercise. Not only that, but during the course of a trial it was not unknown for discovery applications to be made for further documents which had the effect of diverting the parties from concentrating on the real issues. Particularly in cases where large corporations were parties, with numerous departments and with many documents circulating, it was quite easy to identify a particular category of document (even in storage) or a document copied to an obscure individual, which had not been produced for inspection. Some judges did their best to control such applications, but without some powerful weapons in the armoury they were relatively helpless to prevent some of the abuse that took place.

5.11 With that background, some root and branch reform was plainly desirable. The old process of discovery was dismantled and the new process of disclosure under the CPR came into being. The new weapon in the armoury of the court is that the process of disclosure is subject to the overriding objective that the courts must deal with cases justly, described at paras **5.6** and **5.7**.

5.12 There is no question that a fair system of disclosure assists in the just resolution of disputes. The obligation to disclose not only documents which are helpful but also documents which are damaging to one's case is not only salutary but plainly assists all parties in an effective evaluation of the chances of success. The new and important principle for the purpose of disclosure is that such disclosure is restricted to what is necessary in the individual case, and this principle is to be applied rigorously. It will be seen at once that this contrasts with the broader rules under the old concept of discovery.

Standard disclosure

5.13 The order which is normally made is called a 'standard disclosure', and in more complex cases this may be followed by further orders requiring extra disclosure. 'Disclosure' means that a party has to state whether or not a document exists or has existed. The obligation to make disclosure is no longer automatic, but follows upon an order made by the procedural judge at a case-management hearing or upon an application by one of the parties. Once a document has been disclosed, there is a right to inspect the document except where it is no longer in the control of the disclosing party, or where there is some other substantial reason why the document should not be inspected, or where it would be disproportionate to the issue in the case to permit inspection.

What is standard disclosure?

5.14 This requires a party to disclose only those documents on which he relies, and the documents which adversely affect his own case or another person's case, or those which support another person's case. There is a separate category of documents which may be required under a practice direction. Accordingly, it will be apparent that when standard disclosure is ordered, the range of documents which has to be searched for, listed and provided for inspection is radically reduced. Subject to any special order, the documents which are no longer included are those which might be called background documents, ie those of no particular direct relevance. In addition, those documents which came under the heading of 'train of inquiry' are no longer automatically included.

5.15 The expression 'document' has an extended meaning to include anything in which information of any description is recorded. Therefore information on any database is included, as are tape recordings, word processing files and e-mails. It is sound practice as soon as it is realised that there may be a dispute relating to a particular issue for all relevant tapes to be impounded, and for any files or emails to be downloaded and stored. It can be imagined that if it later emerged that any such materials had been deliberately deleted or expunged, the court would be left with a clear impression, absent a suitable explanation, of the destruction of prejudicial matter. The same principle would apply, albeit with less impact, if it emerged that such materials had been allowed to be destroyed through oversight.

Reasonable search

5.16 One of the other features of the new disclosure regime is that while the party giving disclosure plainly has to disclose any document on which it relies, it only has to make a reasonable search for other documents falling within the disclosure categories set out at para **5.14**. Exactly what is reasonable depends upon a number of factors, including the number of documents involved, the nature and complexity of the proceedings, the ease and expense of retrieval of any particular document, and the significance of any document which is likely to be located during the search. If a party has not searched for a particular type of document on the basis that it would be unreasonable to do so, then in the disclosure statement which has to be made this must be stated and the reasons for it must be given.

5.17   The concept of a reasonable search again stresses how the whole concept of disclosure has changed, and how the obligation to disclose has undergone a significant upheaval. Of course there may be very substantial cases where a very broad obligation to search is appropriate. But the underlying key of proportionality has corrected a balance which some felt had gone too far.

5.18   The obligation to make disclosure is limited to those documents which are or have been in a party's control. This means that a party has to disclose a document if it is or was in his physical possession, if he has or has had a right to possession of it, or if he has or has had a right to inspect or take copies of it. If multiple copies of the same document are found, then unless they are marked or altered in some way it is not necessary to disclose more than one copy. As pointed out in para **5.10**, under the old regime this was a real problem for large organisations where many individuals or departments received copies of the same document. Sometimes a department would then re-copy and distribute the document internally or to other office premises. In theory, each copy of the document had to be tracked down and disclosed. It is easier to circulate a document and ask whether or not anyone has a copy which has in any way been marked or altered. The same principles apply to e-mails, although they are of course less likely to have been marked or annotated.

5.19   It will be apparent from the above that there is now far more flexibility within the concept of disclosure. Of course, in an appropriate case a very wide-ranging search may have to be made. If there are large sums of money or other important issues at stake, and if it is a critical part of a case to know who received (or did not receive) a particular piece of information at a particular time (or at all) then a very time-consuming search may have to be made.

Listing the documents

5.20   Once the search has been carried out, in order to comply with the requirements for standard disclosure, the documents which have been located have to be listed in the relevant practice form. The documents are normally listed in a convenient order and manner (for example chronologically, or by subject matter, or by department) and are briefly described. If there is any reason why a particular document should not be disclosed (for example, because there is a duty or right to withhold the document), then it should be stated. Such a right would include documents covered by legal professional privilege: see para **5.27**.

5.21   If the party making the list no longer has a particular document within his control, then he must say so and report what has happened to it. The party making the list must also supply a disclosure statement which sets out the extent of the search that has been made, and the maker's understanding of the duty to disclose, and certifies that such duty has been carried out. The duty to disclose does not end as soon as the search has been made and the list provided. If any further documents emerge which should be disclosed, there is an obligation to disclose those documents until the proceedings are concluded, and the other party should be informed about them as soon as they have come to the notice of the disclosing party.

5.22 It is open to a party to ask the court for an order for specific disclosure or inspection. When considering whether or not to make an order, the court will take account of the overriding objective and the concept of proportionality.

5.23 If a party has a right to inspect a document, then inspection of it has to be permitted. Copies of documents made available for inspection may be made provided the party requesting the copies agrees to pay the supplier's reasonable copying charges.

Public interest immunity

5.24 There are provisions enabling a party to apply to the court without notice (ie the application is made without informing the other parties) for an order that it is entitled to withhold disclosure of a document on the ground that disclosure would damage the public interest. The judge has to balance the public interest in concealment of a document against the public interest in the administration of justice, which requires disclosure so that there can be a fair trial. In addition to this balancing exercise, the requirement for a fair trial under art 6 of the European Convention of Human Rights ('ECHR') also has to be considered.

5.25 It is when the court rules in favour of withholding the material that it is said that the public interest in immunity prevails; ie there is public interest immunity. This used to be known as 'crown privilege', and has been the subject of much development by the courts. There emerged two types of claim for immunity, a 'class' claim, eg for all documents of a particular type, and a 'contents' claim, based upon the contents of a particular document. The former was originally held to succeed only when it was really necessary for the proper functioning of the public service.

5.26 The whole area of public interest immunity was revisited by Sir Richard Scott in his report into the Matrix Churchill prosecution. Partly as a consequence of that report, the courts are extremely cautious in scrutinising class claims and will be unlikely to permit the emergence of any new categories of class claims. An example of a case where such withholding might be sought is where confidential information of a particularly sensitive type has been supplied to the Crown or to a regulatory authority. In the latter case, there is a fair argument for permitting immunity from production only if there is shown to be a clear need to withhold such information from investors.

Legal professional privilege

5.27   One of the problem areas can be the identification of documents which attract legal professional privilege. Privilege is a rule of evidence which entitles a party to withhold production of written or oral evidence during the proceedings. It is this principle which, for example, protects a witness from answering any questions about the legal advice upon which he has acted, unless of course for some reason he has waived privilege (ie agreed that he will forgo his rights not to disclose advice given to him).

5.28   There are two main categories of such privilege. The first is legal advice privilege, which relates to materials which are privileged whether or not litigation is contemplated or pending. The second is litigation privilege, which relates to materials which are privileged only if litigation was contemplated or pending when they were made or came into existence. The latter category is much broader in scope than the former.

5.29   The courts have stressed on many occasions the importance of being able to consult lawyers with absolute confidence that information given to those lawyers or advice received from them is privileged. The privilege is an aspect of the protection of confidentiality, although one of the criticisms of the doctrine is that it is limited to lawyers. Information given in confidence to accountants, doctors and others does not attract such a privilege. The privilege extends only to the obtaining of legal advice and assistance, and all things reasonably necessary in the form of any communication to the lawyers have the benefit of protection from disclosure. The underlying policy is that legal advice must be capable of being sought and given safely without fear of its being produced later in any circumstances (of course there are some exceptions, an obvious one being where proceedings are brought against the lawyers alleging professional negligence, in which case the privilege is waived).

5.30   Provided a particular communication made in confidence between a client and his solicitor, or between the solicitor and his client, is made for the purpose of obtaining or giving legal advice, then the privilege attracted by those documents is a permanent one. One of the practical problems which arises in large organisations is the status of documents sent to or received from the in-house legal department. The privilege extends to all members of the legal profession, and this includes in-house lawyers. A question that sometimes occurs is whether a communication is truly seeking advice from a lawyer acting as such or is seeking some sort of executive action, decision or advice. Merely adding a heading to the effect that a document is privileged will, of course, not render a document privileged if it is not so.

5.31   One of the other points is that solicitors undertake a far wider range of advice and work than simply giving legal advice. They often play more of a commercial role. It is therefore more difficult always to assess whether a particular line of correspondence attracts privilege. The courts have ruled that the test is whether the communication or other document was made confidentially for the purposes of legal advice, and those purposes have to be construed broadly. While in a particular file relating to a transaction there may be few letters actually seeking legal advice as such, the implication is frequently that legal advice should be given if necessary. In addition, it is the lawyer's job to advise on what should prudently and sensibly be done in the legal context (*Balabel v Air India*[1]). One other approach to the question of privilege is to assess whether the retainer (ie the purpose for which the lawyer was retained to act) has as its dominant purpose the obtaining and giving of legal advice. If the answer is yes, then the documents are likely to attract privilege. If, however, the retainer is for a commercial purpose, then it is less likely to attract privilege unless advice is still requested or received.

1   [1988] 2 All ER 246, [1988] Ch 317, CA.

5.32   The second category of privilege arises when litigation is contemplated or pending. This is a wider form of privilege than the first category, but is dependent upon litigation being in existence or pending. Once that point has been reached, then the privilege applies to any communication between the client and his solicitor, or his agent, and indeed applies to any communication written by any of them to any third party. However, the only, or dominant, purpose for which any of those communications must be written is seeking or giving advice in respect of the proceedings or obtaining evidence for use in those proceedings.

5.33   This would cover letters written by a solicitor to a third party dealing, for example, with obtaining evidence or obtaining information which might lead to the obtaining of evidence. For example, a solicitor may wish to obtain a report of a factual nature relating to possible issues in the proceedings and, accordingly, the letter seeking any such information, the attendance notes recording conversations relating to the information, and the report itself, would all be privileged from inspection. There are new rules under the CPR dealing with the obtaining of a view from an expert. Formerly, such documents would be privileged under this head of privilege. However, some documents in respect of the instructions given to an expert are now to be disclosed.

5.34   It is often the case that communications between client and lawyer under this head would have attracted privilege under the legal advice category, but the important extension for litigation privilege is that communication with and from third parties other than the client/lawyer are protected.

5.35 The question of whether or not a document is brought into existence for the dominant purpose of litigation can be a difficult one. For example, there is often an internal enquiry or audit when events have taken place which may lead to litigation. The audit may identify any procedural or operational shortcomings, may include an assessment of whether provision should be made for a claim, and may consider litigation issues. It may also address matters on which legal advice should be sought in case of litigation. What is the dominant purpose of preparing such a report? It is clearly a difficult problem, and the court will apply an objective test, and will not just look at the subjective intention of the author. For example, the author may well be assuming that his report is being produced to ensure a particular procedure is valid; but the real purpose of the report, viewed objectively, may well be for an assessment to be made by lawyers, and advice given by them, as to the risk of litigation.

5.36 However, in the above example the report may well not be privileged, unless the dominant purpose has been addressed with care prior to the writing of the report. If such a report is not privileged, then any documents or materials relied upon by the investigating team would probably have to be disclosed unless there was some counter-argument.

5.37 These principles of legal professional privilege are of general application in civil proceedings. They have been effectively adopted under the FSMA 2000, s 413. This provides that a protected item may not be required to be produced, disclosed or made available for inspection. A protected item is a communication between a person and their professional legal adviser either in connection with the giving of advice to the client or in connection with, or in contemplation of, legal proceedings. There is a broader category of protection when proceedings are contemplated, as is the position under the general law. These principles will be applied in investigations by the Financial Services Authority ('FSA') and in proceedings before the Financial Services and Markets Tribunal. This is considered in para **6.8**, where enforcement procedures are also looked at. Also worthy of mention here is the principle that legal professional privilege does not extend to any document which comes into existence as a step in criminal or illegal proceedings. There must be clear evidence of fraud or illegality to make out such a claim, the effect of which is to destroy privilege, and the courts are reluctant to accede to such a claim without careful consideration. The court will, on the one hand, weigh up the importance of the legal professional privilege, and on the other hand the gravity of whatever type of fraud is alleged to have occurred. Whether the lawyer knew of the fraudulent or illegal purpose does not matter if, in fact, he was being used for that purpose. Under the FSMA 2000, s 413(4) a communication is stated not to be a protected item if it is held with the intention of furthering a criminal purpose.

Privilege against self-incrimination

5.38   This subject is referred to in para **4.69**. The principles apply as much to the production of documents as to the answering of questions. In each case, the rule is that a witness is entitled to refuse to answer any question, or a person is entitled to refuse to produce a document, if the answer or document would have a tendency to expose him (or his spouse) to any criminal charge or penalty. There must be a real risk of such a consequence, rather than an idle or fanciful risk. The underlying principle is that nobody should be compelled by law to give incriminating evidence against himself. Such privilege normally extends to professional disciplinary proceedings, depending upon their nature.

5.39   A number of statutes have abrogated this privilege, particularly in the context of insolvency investigations (referred to in para **4.69**) and in investigations by the Serious Fraud Office. There are issues in this area under the ECHR. The main area where difficulties arise is when a person is obliged to make a statement, and such statement is later deployed in criminal proceedings. This conflicts with the rights accorded under art 6 (right to a fair trial) and the right to remain silent and not incriminate oneself (see para **4.71** on insolvency, and para **4.46** on disclosure in criminal proceedings).

Criminal proceedings

Disclosure in criminal proceedings

5.40   Disclosure in the context of serious criminal proceedings has a different meaning to that used in civil proceedings. In part this is obviously due to the very nature of the different proceedings and the protections required for a person accused of having committed a crime. If a defendant is not obliged to give evidence and is entitled to remain silent when asked questions in interview (albeit there may be consequences in the form of judicial comment and inferences drawn by a jury if he does so), inevitably the shape and nature of the disclosure process in criminal proceedings will be radically different.

5.41   Before the Criminal Procedure and Investigations Act 1996 introduced a new regime of primary and secondary disclosure, the duty on the prosecution to disclose material had been piecemeal. Over the years, the courts increasingly required the prosecution to disclose more and more material to the defence. Such material included witness statements taken from persons who were not to be called to give evidence, statements taken from witnesses which were inconsistent with their later statements, and previous convictions of persons to be called as prosecution witnesses. A number of miscarriages of justice (for example, *R v Ward*[1] concerning the M62 bombing in 1974, although part of the reasoning in that case for allowing the appeal was that government scientists had deliberately withheld evidence because it might damage the prosecution case) and a Royal Commission brought about a more open system of prescribed disclosure.

1   [1993] 2 All ER 577, [1993] 1 WLR 619, CA.

5.42   Under the Criminal Procedure and Investigations Act 1996, there are codes of practice which set out in detail the duties of those who are investigating crime, and the extent of their obligation to retain, record, and hand over to the prosecutor particular materials. Under the rules of primary disclosure, the prosecutor must make disclosure to the defence of any prosecution material which has not already been disclosed and which, in the prosecutor's opinion, might undermine the case for the prosecution against the accused; or he must certify that there is no such material. It will be apparent that it is the subjective view of the prosecutor which determines whether or not materials are to be disclosed.

5.43   There is often a plea and directions hearing at which the court will give directions as to the timetable for disclosure of material. Where primary disclosure has been given, the defence must give a defence statement to the court and to the prosecution. That statement addresses the nature of the defendant's defence, states the matters where there is a dispute with the prosecution and gives the reasons why there is such a dispute. Once that defence statement is received, the prosecution is under a duty to disclose to the accused any prosecution material which has not previously been disclosed to the accused and which might reasonably be expected to assist the accused's defence as disclosed by the defence statement. If there is no such material, then that has to be certified by the prosecution. Under art 6 of the ECHR, the European Court has ruled that the rights in respect of fair trial include a right to disclosure of prosecution materials both for and against the accused.

5.44   Public interest immunity can apply to materials in the possession of the prosecution, and in the event that the prosecution does not wish to disclose such materials, they should make an application to the court for a ruling. Such an application can be made in the absence of the defence. The defence can seek a review in respect of any such ruling, but plainly only if they are aware of the material and any public interest ruling made in respect of it. There will almost certainly be a challenge to the validity of any orders made protecting public interest immunity material under art 6 of the ECHR which gives the right to a fair trial.

Human Rights Act 1998

5.45 Under art 6 of the ECHR, it is provided that in the determination of a person's civil rights and obligations, or of any charge against him, everyone is entitled to a fair and public hearing within a reasonable time by an independent and impartial tribunal established by law. In addition, everyone charged with a criminal offence shall be presumed innocent until proven guilty according to law. This is a very important and evolving area of the law. Although the courts have sometimes stressed that its procedures are already fair, there are certain areas in the criminal field where art 6 has particular impact. By way of example, there is an obligation to make disclosure of prosecution materials, time and facilities have to be granted for the preparation of any defence, and there is a right to a fair and public hearing. The courts have to have regard to any decision of the European Court when making any ruling, and the broad approach of the European Court has extended the apparently simple notion of 'fair trial' to a dynamic and multi-faceted concept.

5.46 The area of particular relevance considered here is the question of self-incrimination. It is addressed in para **4.71** in the context of insolvency. The right to silence is accepted as being part of the right to a fair trial. This is related to, but distinct from, the privilege against self-incrimination dealt with in a civil context at para **5.38**. The critical element is that no person should be obliged to give evidence against themselves in order to admit to guilt. As pointed out in para **5.69**, the normal way in which this can come about is when there is an investigation by such a person as a liquidator. The liquidator, using his powers under the Insolvency Act 1986, compels a person to give evidence, and that evidence includes an admission of guilt to a criminal offence. Can the prosecution rely upon that admission in criminal proceedings? Subject to the powers of the criminal trial judge to exclude such evidence under the Police and Criminal Evidence Act 1984, the answer before the case of *Saunders v United Kingdom*[1] was a qualified 'yes'. The answer now would be rather different. The facts of that case and its implications are dealt with at paras **4.69–4.71**. Whether the courts would still require a party to incriminate himself under such compulsory provisions as the Insolvency Act 1986 is an open question, particularly where the statute contains no safeguard against such use of incriminating material obtained.

1   (1996) 23 EHRR 313, [1998] 1 BCLC 362.

Freezing orders

5.47 In 1975 the courts began to make orders preventing foreign defendants from removing their assets from the jurisdiction. This was a novel idea, and in the first few cases defendants who were resident out of the jurisdiction but who had a bank account located in England could be stopped even before judgement from removing those funds. The application to freeze all or part of the bank account was made by the claimant without notifying the defendant. One of the first cases was called *Mareva Compania Naviera SA v International Bulkcarriers SA*[1]. From this case the new form of injunction took its name: 'The Mareva'. When the civil procedure reforms came into force in 1999, this became a 'freezing order'.

1   [1975] 2 Lloyd's Rep 509.

5.48   The test which the court applied when considering making one of these orders was that if it appeared that a debt was due and owing and there was a danger that the debtor might dispose of his assets so as to defeat the claimant's case before judgement, the court would in a proper case grant an interlocutory injunction. The underlying principle was that if the court did not interfere by injunction then the claimants would suffer a grave injustice which the court had power to help avoid.

5.49   From these relatively small beginnings, the jurisdiction created by the courts slowly grew. For a few years the courts did not grant Mareva orders restraining the removal of assets of persons resident within England and Wales. Gradually, the courts extended the scope of the orders, making them against those resident in the jurisdiction but temporarily absent abroad. Parliament recognised the general principle of the Mareva order in the Supreme Court Act 1981, s 37(3).

5.50   The nature of the order was gradually extended to prevent the dissipation of assets within the jurisdiction, as well as the removal of assets from the jurisdiction, and this was in respect of persons resident within the jurisdiction. The court was extremely careful to ensure that there was a 'good arguable case' in terms of the underlying claim, and generally required to be satisfied that there was a real risk that the defendants would remove their assets from the jurisdiction or otherwise dispose of them if an injunction was not granted.

5.51   Another extension took place in 1989 when the courts started to make orders in respect of assets which were themselves outside the jurisdiction. This of course gave rise to a number of difficulties in terms of restraining acts which might be otherwise lawful in other jurisdictions and which indeed might be the subject of a contrary order by the local courts. Another difficult area is whether third parties (eg a foreign bank or other institution holding assets of a defendant whose assets have been frozen) would be bound by the order of an English court in an action to which it is not a party.

5.52   The Mareva or freezing order was sought in a wide range of cases, and indeed at one stage was too frequently sought and granted. A successful claimant would, in a typical case, give notice of the order to a defendant's bankers. The effect of this would be to bind the bank, since if a third party had notice of the order and took any steps which might be said to aid and abet a breach of the injunction, that third party was itself in contempt of court. Once a bank had been given such notice, clearly it regarded its customer in a rather different way, and indeed sometimes the very act of informing the bank was itself somewhat oppressive if the sums involved were not large. Another consideration is that a party's assets could be effectively frozen for some time until the action had been heard or until some compromise had been reached.

5.53 This judge-made area of the law, with its enormous implications for parties, was subject to constant refinement, and eventually to practice directions from the court setting out in detail the procedure for obtaining such orders. These directions set out standard forms for the injunctions to avoid the omission of important safeguards for a defendant. These included the undertakings which the claimant has to give to the court. If a claimant breaches any of those undertakings, it may itself be liable for contempt.

5.54 The claimant has to undertake to commence proceedings if it has not already done so. It has to serve upon the defendant the claim form and other documents setting out the claim, the evidence and a copy of the order made as soon as practicable. It has to give an undertaking to the court that if the order should not have been made it will (if the court so orders) pay compensation to the defendant for any losses suffered by it by reason of the order. Sometimes the claimant will have to furnish security to back such an undertaking. The claimant also has to agree to pay the reasonable costs of any third party served with copies of the order which are caused by the order. For example, a bank which is served with a copy of the order will have to make checks to see whether an identifiable account should be frozen, and may have to spend time identifying any other account or assets which should be frozen.

5.55 One of the other main controls used by the court is the obligation on the part of the claimant to make full and frank disclosure to the court when making the application. This is a duty which applies to all claimants who seek injunctive relief without the defendant being present, and the reasons for this duty are obvious. The court is making an order which may have far-reaching consequences, and needs to be as sure as possible that it has all the relevant facts for the purpose of ensuring that it is acting justly and with fairness. Such a duty of disclosure extends to the nature of the claimant's claim, and any possible weaknesses or defences that are known to the claimant. Another area where there has to be full disclosure is the ability of the claimant to satisfy any award made to the defendant under the undertaking in damages. A failure to comply with the duty to make full disclosure is treated very seriously by the court, and can result in the order being discharged and an order being made for the claimant to pay costs, and also compensation to the defendant for the order having been made in the first place.

5.56   The type of safeguard built into the order itself also addresses such matters as (in the case of a business) permitting that business to continue to operate by the payment of proper business expenses, subject to appropriate safeguards. The payment of legal expenses is also allowed subject to suitable limits.

5.57   One of the areas which can give rise to difficulties is when the court makes an order requiring the defendant to swear an affidavit disclosing his assets, giving their location value and the details of the same. Other orders can also be made requiring the defendant to give details regarding what has happened to certain assets or money which the claimant is trying to trace.

5.58   When such an order is made there can be problems because the defendant is not obliged to incriminate himself, although there are some statutory exceptions, for example in respect of passing off or for the infringement of intellectual property rights such as patents, trademarks, copyright and confidential information. Under the Theft Act 1968, s 31, the privilege against self-incrimination is withdrawn when proceedings are brought, for example, to recover property, and there is a risk that the person who has to make an affidavit may be prosecuted for an offence under the Theft Act itself.

5.59   The court may also make search orders, whereby the owner of property is prevented by the court from refusing entry to persons who are seeking evidence for a particular purpose. These orders were originally called 'Anton Piller' orders after the case where they were devised. These orders were very popular for a time, but were open to abuse. They could also be very intimidating to home occupiers who were suddenly confronted with a number of lawyers who had come to execute orders which a lay person might find confusing in terminology. The courts developed the idea of an independent solicitor being present effectively to police execution of the order and to make a report to the court. Although they are still made, they are not nearly as frequent now. There is a watered down version of the order, whereby nobody enters the particular building under the terms of an order, but the occupier has to deliver up particular documents at the door of the building.

5.60   Similar problems arise to those met with freezing orders when the courts add disclosure orders requiring the defendant to state what has happened to a particular asset. These are the problems of self-incrimination dealt with in para **5.38**. There may be issues under the Human Rights Act 1998 under these orders. For example, under art 8 of the ECHR there is the right to respect for a person's private and family life, his home and his correspondence. Balanced against this is the fact that some interference with those rights is accepted as being necessary in a democratic society in the interests of national security, public safety, or for the prevention of disorder or crime, for the protection of public order, health and morals, or for the protection of the rights and freedoms of others.

5.61   It will be immediately apparent that the making of orders requiring disclosure under order of the court may well raise issues under art 8 of the ECHR, and the court when considering making such an order will have to evaluate the evidence placed before it with a view to the requirements of the ECHR. If there is a strong case showing the infringement of the claimant's rights, and demonstrating that those rights have to be protected by the making of a suitable disclosure order, then the court will no doubt weigh up those arguments having regard to the nature of the case which emerges before it at the stage where one party only is present.

CHAPTER 6

Enforcement – pre-trial, trial and disciplinary

6.1 This chapter deals with the Financial Services and Markets Tribunal ('the Tribunal'), which will have extensive powers in a number of situations. For example, it will be able to deal with market abuse and alleged breaches of Listing Rules where a person has received a decision notice from the Financial Services Authority ('FSA') and has referred the matter to the Tribunal. It will also deal with such matters as the giving, the variation and the revocation of permissions by the FSA. There is a right on the part of an aggrieved person in such circumstances to refer the matter to the Tribunal. If the FSA comes to the conclusion that a person is not a fit and proper person to perform functions in respect of a regulated activity carried out by an authorised person, then a person against whom a decision is made to make a prohibition order may refer the matter to the Tribunal.

6.2 While the Tribunal has very extensive powers over a wide range of circumstances, the procedural rules under which it will operate (themselves at the draft stage at the time of writing) have plainly been drafted with an eye to the Human Rights Act 1998, and to art 6 of the European Convention on Human Rights ('ECHR').

6.3 The applicant has to initiate any proceedings by filing at the Tribunal a reference notice, which is to be signed by him or by his representative. This has to be done within 28 days of the notice served upon the applicant by the FSA, which itself gives rise to the reference. There are provisions for extending the time for making the application. Within the reference notice the applicant may seek an order that no particulars about the reference should be entered in the register, and suspension of the FSA's action pending determination of the issues by the Tribunal.

6.4 The applicant sends a copy of the reference notice to the FSA. At the Tribunal, the reference notice, once received, will be logged. Normally, the FSA should then file its written statement, to be known, as in the civil courts, as its 'statement of case'. That is to be done within 28 days. The statement of case sets out all of the facts and matters relied upon by the FSA to support the action taken by it, the statutory provisions under which the action is taken, and the reasons for taking the referred action at all. Again, there are provisions enabling extensions of time to be given by the Tribunal, which it can order provided it is satisfied that it is in the interests of justice to do so.

6.5   Once the applicant has received the statement of case, it has to file a written reply setting out the grounds on which it relies in its reference, identify all of the matters in the statement of case which are in dispute, and state the reasons for such dispute. Twenty-eight days is allowed for the sending of the reply, a copy of which is to be sent to the FSA. Extensions of time can be ordered if it is in the interests of justice to do so.

6.6   There is automatic disclosure under the rules which takes place upon the sending of the reply by the applicant. At the same time as sending his reply, he has to send a list of the documents on which he relies in support of his case. Within 21 days thereafter, the FSA has to send a list of the documents on which it relied when deciding to give the notice which has given rise to the reference. It also has to send a list including any material which, in the opinion of the FSA, might undermine that decision, or might reasonably be expected to assist the applicant's case as disclosed by the applicant's reply (this is similar to the new test for disclosure under the CPR 31.6).

6.7   The rules provide that no document need be included in the list if it has been intercepted under the terms of any warrant relating to the interception of communications, or if it indicates that such a warrant has been issued or that a document has been intercepted under the terms of a warrant. Applications for interception warrants may be made by a list of specified authorities (for example, the Director General of the National Criminal Intelligence Service) under the Regulation of Investigatory Powers Act 2000.

6.8   Any document which is listed is to be made available to the other party for copying, or a copy may be supplied. Excluded from documents to be made available are protected items, ie those which attract legal professional privilege. Protected items are defined under the Financial Services and Markets Act 2000 ('FSMA 2000'), s 413. They include documents which seek or contain legal advice, and documents seeking or containing legal advice or communications with third parties if they come into being for the purpose of proceedings when legal proceedings are contemplated or are in being.

6.9   The FSA is entitled to withhold disclosure if it relates to a third party's case which the FSA took into account for the purpose of comparison. Also, the FSA may decline disclosure if the document should not be shown because it would not be in the public interest, or it would not be fair having regard to the likely significance of the document to the applicant, and the possible prejudice which may be caused to the commercial interests of a person other than the applicant. The Tribunal may give directions in respect of a document. The draft rules do not address the difficulties which may be encountered by the FSA in trying to decide whether or not any item is indeed a protected item or whether it should, in fact, be disclosed. There may be developed or prescribed a procedure similar to that in criminal proceedings where a judge considers a document in the presence of one party only and makes a ruling upon whether it should be disclosed. Subject to the above, the Tribunal may order that a document which is in the custody of either party and which the Tribunal considers to be of relevance or possible relevance to the reference is to be disclosed.

6.10   The applicant may withdraw its application without permission unless the hearing has commenced, in which case it would require the permission of the Tribunal. The FSA can, of course, decide no longer to oppose an application. There are rules enabling the Tribunal in certain limited circumstances to make appropriate orders if, for example, an application is no longer opposed, or if no statement of case is filed in time. The applicant has to be given notice of any such intention of dismissing the application so that it can make representations. Costs orders can be made in such circumstances.

6.11   The Tribunal is permitted to make orders which will enable the hearing to run smoothly, and to help the Tribunal determine the issues and to ensure the just, expeditious and economical determination of the reference. Directions may provide for an oral hearing, and may order a party to give more information about its case. An order may be made requiring a party to supply a list of issues and facts, and identifying those issues or facts which are or are not agreed. Orders may be made requiring a party to give a list of the witnesses which it proposes to call at the hearing, and to file witness statements in respect of those witnesses. Orders may also be made providing for the manner in which evidence can be given (eg videolink), and the appointment of an expert to assist the Tribunal.

6.12   The Tribunal may order that action taken by the FSA be suspended provided the applicant has filed a reference notice. This is obviously to prevent any injustice by the premature operation of an action prior to its consideration by the Tribunal. The Tribunal may suspend such action provided it is satisfied that to do so would not prejudice (a) the interests of any persons, including consumers, investors or otherwise, intended to be protected by the proposed action; and (b) the smooth operation of any market intended to be protected by the referred action. The FSA has to be permitted to make representations if an application for suspension is made.

6.13   If different references relate to the same matter, or relate to separate interests in respect of the same matter, or simply involve the same issues, then the Tribunal has power to order that the references be consolidated together.

6.14 The Tribunal may issue a witness summons and require the attendance of a witness at a particular time and place to give evidence as a witness, and may also order that particular documents be produced by that witness if the Tribunal considers it necessary to examine such a document. Excluded from this are, of course, protected documents, as discussed in para **6.8**, or those documents which a party would be able to claim it had a right or duty not to disclose.

6.15 The Tribunal may order a preliminary hearing in order to decide particular issues, for example any matter of fact or law which might be helpfully resolved at an early stage. Indeed, if it appears that the resolution of such issues disposed substantially of the reference, the Tribunal could choose to treat the preliminary hearing as the hearing of the reference itself. Such hearings may be resolved without an oral hearing, but no disposal of the reference may be made without an oral hearing unless the parties have agreed to the same in writing.

6.16 If the matter proceeds to a full hearing, then the time and place for the hearing are communicated to the parties. Again, there is provision for matters to proceed (with the consent of the parties) without an oral hearing. While the normal rule is that all hearings are to be conducted in public, all or part of a hearing may be directed to be held in private upon the application of a party if it is considered to be in the interests of morals, public order, national security, or the protection of the private lives of the parties, and any unfairness to the applicant or prejudice to the interests of consumers that might result from a hearing in public. In either case, the Tribunal has to be satisfied that a hearing in private would not prejudice the interests of justice.

6.17 The parties are entitled to appear at the hearing, and are entitled to be represented by any person, whether legally qualified or not. The FSMA 2000, s 134 makes provision for a legal assistance scheme for individuals, subject to the making of regulations by the Lord Chancellor. The parties are also entitled to assistance from any person if they require it. The Tribunal is empowered (although presumably extreme circumstances would be required) to refuse to permit a person to assist or represent a party at a hearing. If a party fails to attend, the Tribunal is free to make an order if it is satisfied that there is no good and sufficient reason for the absence. If an order is made in the absence of one of the parties, then the absent party may apply to have the order varied or set aside in certain circumstances.

6.18 At the hearing the parties may give evidence, call witnesses, question any witnesses, and address the Tribunal generally on the evidence and on the reference. While evidence can be given by affidavit or written statement, the Tribunal may decide that it requires the attendance of the maker of such a written statement. No expert evidence is to be adduced by a party without the consent of the Tribunal. The Tribunal is not constrained by any rules of evidence, and is able to hear of matters which were not known to the FSA at the time of the making of its decision.

6.19   The decision of the Tribunal is to be reduced to writing, unless all or part of the hearing was held in private. In that case the Tribunal may make amendments to the text of its ruling, as it considers necessary. Orders for costs may be made by the Tribunal, either of a fixed amount, or of such sum as may be assessed. There is a power to review the decision made if, for example, new evidence has become available or if the interests of justice so require. Appeals are made to the Court of Appeal, but permission is required from the Tribunal. If that permission is refused, then an appropriate application has to be made to the Court of Appeal.

CHAPTER 7

Overseas regulators and mutual assistance

7.1 In this chapter the existing and developing relationship between regulators overseas and the Financial Services Authority ('FSA') will be explored. Under the Financial Services and Markets Act 2000 ('the FSMA 2000'), other UK legislation and EU Directives there are a number of provisions that will facilitate the exchange of information between enforcement agencies and regulators within the EU and globally. The problems that have arisen in the recent past have frequently centred on the question of jurisdiction and whether the offence subject to an investigation has a comparable status within the country providing assistance. The issue of mutual assistance is dealt with under a number of sections within the FSMA 2000, and it is clear that the legislature has sought to clarify the law and provide a framework that will make it easier in the future for agencies to exchange information and conduct enquiries on behalf of overseas regulators.

7.2 The chapter is divided into four parts. In the first part there is a discussion of the law from the perspective of domestic legislation, that is under the FSMA 2000, and also other relevant acts such as the Criminal Justice Act 1993 ('CJA 1993'), Parts I–VI and the Criminal Justice (International Co-operation) Act 1990 ('CJICA 1990'). The second part of the chapter focuses on the Directives that have emanated from the EU and also the work of The Forum of European Securities Commission ('FESCO'). Part three of the chapter covers the international perspective and the work of The International Organisation of Securities Commissions ('IOSCO'), and briefly looks at the provisions that exist for the exchange of information from a number of specific countries as well as commenting upon the way the law has developed in Canada where decisions of the higher courts are not binding in the UK but are nevertheless persuasive. The chapter concludes with a look at future developments and consideration of potential models for a global regulator.

Domestic provisions for mutual assistance

7.3   The basis of assisting overseas regulators or investigating authorities is reciprocity. It is recognised that behaviour may take place within or outside of the UK that may have an adverse effect on home or host state financial markets, and it is therefore in the interests of all market participants to co-operate and ensure the exchange of information between authorities to ensure that appropriate enforcement action is taken against abusive market behaviour.

7.4   Requests for assistance may be either incoming from overseas or outgoing from the FSA to an overseas authority. Incoming requests can be divided into two categories: assistance under Community obligations, and other requests. In respect of any Community request, it must first be established that there is an obligation; assuming this to be the case then the FSA must satisfy itself that there are sufficient grounds for it to exercise its powers.

7.5   Interestingly, when considering the effect of the FSA in exercising its powers, any decisions that it comes to are of course challengeable through the Financial Services Tribunal ('the Tribunal'). As Michael Blair points out[1]:

> 'Since these cases are also referable ... the existence of the Community obligation, and the basis on which the home regulator had acted if relevant, will be capable of judicial reconsideration.'

1   Blair, M Minghella, L et al *Blackstone's Guide to the Financial Services and Markets Act 2000*, 'Incoming Firms: Intervention by the FSA', (2001), p 173.

7.6   It is therefore the case that market participants may well see evidence of action being taken by the FSA on behalf of overseas regulators even though the circumstances of the actions do amount to an offence itself under the FSMA 2000. One such example of this would be in cases of market abuse where behaviour conducted outside of the UK may damage the integrity of the UK markets. In these circumstances the FSA will consider whether it is appropriate to impose a fine or issue a public statement in addition to providing assistance to the home regulator. At some point in the proceedings the FSA will then make a strategic decision as to whether or not it will take the lead role in bringing a criminal prosecution or a supportive role in facilitating the supply of documentary and oral evidence.

7.7   The FSMA 2000, Part VI (permission to carry on regulated activities) applies to all firms. As such, s 47, which is contained within this Part, enables the FSA to cancel or vary permission on its own initiative on behalf of an overseas regulator. The Treasury is empowered to prescribe the sort of overseas authority that the FSA should assist, and these include those overseas bodies that have functions similar to those of the FSA, the competent authority for listing, the Secretary of State under the

FSMA 2000 and prosecuting authorities for money laundering and insider dealing[1].

1   Those readers who have found it necessary to look at the complete provisions of the FSMA 2000, s 47 will note that the reference to 'request' in sub-s (7) only applies to sub-s (5) and not sub-ss (4) and (5). This is an error and is recognised in the *Explanatory Notes: Financial Services and Markets Act 2000, Chapter 8* (2000) HMSO, p 29, para 112.

7.8   The FSA is committed to providing all assistance possible to European Economic Area ('EEA') Competent Authorities and to these ends it has stated that[1]:

'The FSA views such co-operation and collaboration as essential to effective regulation of the international market in financial services. It will therefore exercise its *own-initiative power* wherever:

- an EEA Competent Authority requests it to do so; and
- it is satisfied that the use of the power is appropriate to enforce effectively the regulatory requirements imposed pursuant to the *Single Market Directives* or other Community obligations (original emphasis).'

1   *The Enforcement Manual: Draft Manual*, Consultation Paper 65a (2000) FSA, ENF Chapter 4, p 10, para 4.6.21.

7.9   Throughout the FSMA 2000 there are a number of references to the policy that the FSA will adopt in exercising its power to conduct investigations on behalf of overseas regulators, as well as specific requirements relating to requests that the FSA can make of regulators outside of the UK. Under the FSMA 2000, s 169 the FSA has obtained powers similar to those available to the Department of Trade and Industry under s 82 of the Companies Act 1989 ('CA 1989'), whereby at the request of an overseas regulator the FSA may exercise the power conferred on it under the FSMA 2000, s 165, that is give notice to an authorised person that it requires information and documents, or the FSA may appoint one or more competent persons to investigate the matter on behalf of an overseas regulator. If this second course of action is taken then any inspector appointed has exactly the same powers as he would have if appointed by the FSA to investigate a domestic regulatory matter.

7.10   Additionally, if the request is from an EU regulator, ie a Competent Authority, then the FSA must, in deciding whether or not to exercise its investigative powers, consider whether it is obliged to exercise such powers in order that it fulfils any Community obligation to do so[1]. What this means is that the FSA does not have to give consideration to all of the criteria that it is required to exercise when considering giving support to a request for assistance from an overseas regulator who is not an EU authority.

1   For example, obligations under the First Banking Co-ordination Directive, the Credit Institutions Directive (formerly contained within the Second Banking Co-ordination Directive), various Insurance Directives and, most significantly, the Investment Services Directive. Each of these imposes an obligation on Competent Authorities to co-operate and provide mutual assistance in the discharge of their functions.

7.11   In all other cases the FSA will base its decision on whether to give assistance on the following factors:

- whether, in the requesting jurisdiction, comparable support would be given to an FSA request for assistance;
- whether the breach of law alleged has a close parallel in the UK;
- the seriousness of the case and its importance to persons in the UK; and
- whether it is in the public interest to give the assistance requested.

Section 169(5) of the FSMA 2000 provides that, except for EU Competent Authorities, the FSA may decline to exercise its powers unless the requesting overseas authority undertakes to make a contribution towards the FSA's costs.

7.12   If the FSA decides to exercise its authority and appoint an investigator on behalf of an overseas regulator, then that overseas regulator may be permitted to attend and take part in any interviews; this is euphemistically known as the 'sitting in' direction. This proviso is subject to the FSA being satisfied that any protections that exist under UK law, to ensure that there are safeguards relating to the use and disclosure of information obtained, are protected by equivalent provisions in the requesting state. The meaning of the term 'overseas regulator' is defined in the FSMA 2000, s 195 and corresponds to functions undertaken by the FSA, the DTI under the Companies Act 1985, and any authority that has the function of investigating insider dealing and market abuse, whether determined as a criminal offence or not within the requesting state.

7.13   Part XIII of the FSMA 2000 deals with the intervention of incoming firms by the FSA. This Part confers on the FSA and the Director General of Fair Trading ('DGFT') the power to intervene in the business of certain firms who are authorised either by way of passport rights or Treaty rights. Under the passport rights provision all EU states, plus Norway, Iceland and Liechtenstein, have the right to carry on investment business in any other member state due to their home state authorisation[1].

1   For a full overview of the provisions see the FSMA 2000, Sch 3.

7.14   Treaty rights refer to the rights that go beyond those covered by the Single Market Directives as defined in Sch 3 of the FSMA 2000. Treaty rights are such that persons who are authorised in their home state may conduct business in any other member state provided that the relevant law of the home state provides equivalent protections to that of the host state.

7.15   Now, it may appear that these provisions do little more than the passporting rights discussed in paras **7.8** and **7.9**, but the difference is that the Directives to which passport rights apply do not cover the full range of financial services that may be offered. Consequently it has been necessary to create a mechanism whereby a financial service provider from one member state can exercise all their rights in the absence of a relevant passport right. This is achieved through the Treaty Rights provision[1].

1   See the FSMA 2000, Sch 4.

7.16   The statutory power to assist is contained within the FSMA 2000, s 195, which virtually mirrors the provisions of s 47 of the FSMA 2000 in respect of the obligation placed upon the FSA to decide whether or not to exercise its discretion and assist dependent upon whether or not the requesting state is an EEA or other overseas authority[1]. The only difference between the sections is that s 195 does not apply to those persons who are authorised solely due to Part VI permission or the additional Part VI permissions that some incoming firms may hold. Section 195 does apply to all regulated activities that have qualified for authorisation under Schs 3 and 4.

1   This is confirmed under the FSMA 2000, s 196: 'This section provides that the nature and extent of the Authority's power of intervention are the same as the power to vary permission or impose a requirement under Part VI'.

7.17   The FSA is required to follow procedural guidelines when it proposes to exercise its powers in respect of incoming firms; these are the same as those contained under the FSMA 2000, s 53 which require the FSA to give written notice of any proposed variations and the date on which it takes effect. The FSA must also inform the recipient of their right to make representations to the FSA and have the matter referred to the Tribunal. Similar provisions apply in respect of the service of warning notices and decision notices in cases of cancellation of permission[1].

1   These are also similar to the safeguards contained within the FSMA 2000, s 54 and attract the same rights as those set out in ss 393 and 394 ('third party rights and access to authority material').

7.18   The FSA may also act on behalf of an insurance authority in another EEA state, and in this capacity as host state; it may apply to the courts for an injunction to freeze the assets held in the UK by the home state insurance firm[1]. In order to assist in this way it is necessary for the home state to show that the insurance firm has failed to comply with requirements under a number of the provisions contained within the 1st Life Directive[2].

1   FSMA 2000, s 198.
2   Failure to comply with a requirement under arts 15, 16(3), 17, and 20, or art 17 of the 1st Non-Life Directive.

7.19   In certain cases the FSA may require that the home state take action against an incoming firm. Typically this would occur where an EEA firm has contravened an FSA requirement that is one which the home state might also apply. If the FSA considers that the appropriate action has not been taken or the measures taken by the home state regulator are inadequate then the FSA may choose to exercise its powers of intervention. Clearly this is a fairly drastic measure as it amounts to a vote of no confidence in the home state regulator. Therefore before the FSA takes such action it is subject to approval from the European Commission, and the FSA must make any amendments to the proposed action that the European Commission stipulates[1].

1   FSMA 2000, s 199.

7.20 There are a limited number of restrictions on the range of actions that the FSA can seek to take against an incoming firm where it feels the host state has failed to remedy a problem. For example, the FSA cannot petition for the winding up of an incoming EEA or Treaty firm unless it has been requested to do so by the home state regulator[1]. Quite understandably, this is because it is felt that the implications of winding up are principally the concern of a home state and it would not be appropriate to transfer this responsibility to a host state regulator.

1   FSMA 2000, s 368.

Third country decisions

7.21 Part XXVIII of the FSMA 2000 deals with a number of miscellaneous matters including reciprocity powers. Under a number of EC Directives[1] the Commission or Council of the EU may make decisions relating to depriving subsidiaries of firms that are outside of the EEA from having access to EEA financial markets. When such a decision is taken it is referred to as a 'Third Country Decision'. The basis for making a decision is where there is evidence to the effect that an EEA firm who is seeking to establish itself in a non-EEA state is receiving less favourable treatment than that home state's own financial providers. If this is found to be the case then, in response, the Commission or Council may issue a decision[2].

1   Investment Services Directive, art 7(5), 2nd Banking Co-ordination Directive, art 9(4), 1st Non-Life Insurance Directive, art 29b(4), and 1st Life Insurance Directive, art 32b(4).
2   Since 1 March 1999, decision action is limited to those countries who are *not* members of the World Trade Organisations as, since this date, the EU has committed itself to permanent recognition of 'Most Favoured Nation' treatment to all WTO members and, accordingly, such action as issuing a decision would not be in accordance with this commitment.

7.22 Section 405 of the FSMA 2000 defines what action is to be taken in the event of a decision being issued. On notification from the Treasury the FSA may refuse an application from a third country, defer its decision to grant an application indefinitely or for a specified period of time, give notice of its objection to a person who has notified of his intention to acquire 50% or more of a controlling interest in a UK authorised person, or give notice of its objection to a person who has acquired a 50% stake in an authorised person[1].

1   The FSMA 2000, s 405(1)(a), (b), (c), (d). In respect of (d), the objection notice may be served irrespective of whether the required notice of control, as required under Pt XII, sub-ss (1)(c) and (d), has been served or not. In addition, under sub-s (2) a direction may be given to any person who falls within a class specified in the direction and a direction may be given in respect of any future applications.

7.23 It is important to note that if a third country subsidiary firm already has passport rights in an EU state then it is not affected by Third Country Decisions. However, this does not extend to third country subsidiary firms who are authorised in EEA states that are not EU states, ie Norway, Iceland and Liechtenstein[1]. Gibraltar also has a special status under the FSMA 2000, s 409, which permits the Treasury to extend Sch 3 status to Gibraltar firms in order that they can qualify for authorised firm status within the UK, and also attract the reciprocal treatment from all other EEA states as afforded to UK firms[2].

1 Firms falling within this category are referred to as 'EFTA firms' (FSMA 2000, s 408(8)).
2 FSMA 2000, s 409.

7.24 The final section of note under the miscellaneous provisions is the FSMA 2000, s 410. This section grants a general power on the Treasury to order a number of bodies to take, or refrain from taking, specific action that may be incompatible with any UK Community or international obligations. For example[1], if the UK's obligations under EC law were not being fulfilled as a result of the FSA's rules on capital requirements, s 410 of the FSMA 2000 permits the Treasury to direct the FSA to change its rules to ensure compliance.

1 As cited in the Explanatory Notes, section 410, p 134.

Other domestic provisions

7.25 Under the FSMA 2000 the FSA has a general responsibility to assist in the prevention and detection of specific and general financial crimes. The level of assistance that it gives is unconditional provided that it is legally permissible to exchange the information. This very broad provision apparently has no jurisdictional boundaries either as[1]:

> 'The Authority must take such steps as it considers appropriate to co-operate with other persons (whether in the United Kingdom or elsewhere) who have functions: (a) similar to those of the Authority; or (b) in relation to the prevention or detection of financial crime.'

1 FSMA 2000, s 354 which goes on to say: '(2) Co-operation may include the sharing of information which the Authority is not prevented from disclosing'. Financial crime has the same, now familiar, meaning as defined in the FSMA 2000, s 6.

7.26 The implications of this section are such that it is now necessary to look outside of the FSMA 2000 to consider where and how under domestic legislation the FSA may further facilitate the exchange of information between overseas investigation and enforcement agencies.

7.27 In 1999 Howard Davies commented that the interests of the London markets would be best served by a regulatory regime based on criminal procedures[1]. A fundamental feature of this has been to recognise certain conduct as criminal in nature in order that those suspected of committing financial crimes may be successfully prosecuted by the state that has been affected by the criminal action. To a large extent this has been achieved through provisions enacted under the FSMA 2000. In addition, these have been supplemented by retaining a number of the measures contained within the Financial Services Act 1986 ('FSA 1986') and the CA 1989, and by bringing into force Part I of the CJA 1993 and making amendments to the CJICA 1990. These Acts will now be discussed within the context of mutual assistance between the FSA and overseas agencies.

1   Howard Davies 'The FSA One Year On', speech delivered 16 June 1999. Available at fsa.gov.uk/pubs/press.

7.28   The new regime for the regulation of the financial service sector has brought about radical changes. However, the implementation of the FSMA 2000 represents one of many strands of legislation, and a number of earlier provisions remain in place to complement the facilitation of cross border assistance. Under the FSMA 2000, Sch 2(7):

> 'The organisation must be able and willing to promote and maintain high standards of integrity and fair dealing in the carrying on of investment business and to co-operate, by the sharing of information and otherwise, with the Secretary of State and any other authority, body or person having responsibility for the supervision or regulation of investment business or other financial services.'

These words are reiterated under Sch 7(5) in relation to the formation of the Securities Investment Board as a designated agency under the FSA 1986.

7.29   Under the FSA 1986, s 179 it is permissible to disclose information to an overseas authority subject to the approval of the person from whom the information was obtained[1]. This restriction is not absolute though as under the FSA 1986, s 180(1)(qq): 'Section 179 shall not preclude the disclosure of information for the purpose of enabling or assisting an overseas regulator to exercise its regulatory authority'[2] and may not inhibit the exercise of any obligations that the UK has under Community law. These provisions are ancillary to the general power contained within the FSA 1986, s 105 that permit an investigation into the affairs of any person carrying on investment business in the UK[3].

1   FSA 1986, s 179(5).
2   These provisions have been subject to amendments under the CA 1989.
3   There are many similarities between the FSA 1986, the CA 1989 and the FSMA 2000. The previous legislation was, in some senses, rather restrictive in terminology; for example which documents could be taken for inspection and who within an organisation might be required to provide information. Also, it was not clear as to what precise requirement there was to disclose information under Community obligations. This has now been clarified and is for all useful purposes a mandatory, not discretional, requirement. For further commentary see Watson, J 'International Co-Operation in the Field of Financial Regulatory Enforcement, Part 1, The UK Approach', *Butterworths Journal of International Banking and Financial Law* (December 1999), pp 467–470.

7.30 A number of matters legislated for under the FSA 1986 were amended by the CA 1989, which came into force in February 1990. International co-operation matters were subject to amendments that reflected growing concerns over the volume of international frauds that were committed through the utilisation of new technologies, and in particular e-crimes. Sections 82–91 of the CA 1989 brought in a range of measures to ease the exchange of information and permit the Secretary of State to order an investigation on behalf of an overseas authority[1].

1   The powers under the CA 1989, ss 82 and 83 permit the Secretary of State to demand the production of documents and any person for interview on behalf of the requesting overseas state.

7.31 Increasing awareness of the threat posed to the city by international fraudsters, particularly through the use of electronic commerce, prompted a Law Commission report into 'Jurisdiction over offences of fraud and dishonesty with a foreign element'[1]. The report recommended a series of reforms to the rules relating to jurisdiction in fraud and dishonesty-related offences. These reforms translated into the CJA 1993, the majority of which finally came into force in 2000.

1   Law Commission Report No 180, London, HMSO, 27 April 1989.

7.32 The CJA 1993, inter alia, makes provision about the jurisdiction of the courts in England and Wales in relation to certain offences of dishonesty and blackmail. It implements the provisions of the Community Council Directive No 89/592/EEC to amend and restate the law about insider dealing, it provides for certain offences created by the Banking Co-ordination (Second Council Directive) Regulations 1992 (SI 1992/3218) to make these offences punishable in the same way as offences under ss 39, 40 and 41 of the Banking Act 1987.

7.33 In relation to the offences mentioned, the relevant act for the purposes of jurisdiction means any act, omission or other event; and any question as to where it occurred is to be disregarded[1]. A person may be guilty of a Group A or Group B offence whether or not he is a British citizen or whether he was in England or Wales at any such time[2].

1   CJA 1993, Pt I, s 2(2).
2   CJA 1993, Pt I, s 3(1)(a), (b).

7.34 Not surprisingly, fraud frequently features as a cross-border crime. Whereas crimes of physical violence require a real proximity of victim and defendant[1], deception offences do not. As a result of greater Internet participation, it can be anticipated that international financial centres will experience a significant increase in the volume of financial frauds, market abuse and money laundering offences that they are exposed to.

1   It is accepted that within this example it is quite possible for a defendant to shoot a victim across an international border and, in doing so, a cross-border offence of physical violence would have been committed.

7.35   It is therefore crucial that legislation is in place to ease the process by which information can be exchanged and multi-jurisdictional prosecutions can be brought[1]. The provisions of the CJA 1993 go some way towards facilitating this whilst respecting the premise that criminal law has traditionally been the preserve of the domestic legislature[2].

1   Legislation is not the only route through which this can be achieved, and commonly there have been agreements between countries to prosecute or exchange information in the state where the actions of the suspect have had some effect, eg some of the 'Boiler Room' prosecutions brought against US and Canadian defendants in a number of EU states during the late 1980s.
2   It is recognised that the number of international criminal offences is increasing whereby, irrespective of where the offence took place, any nation state can claim jurisdiction and the right to prosecute.

7.36   One interesting feature related to increasing international comity is that the FSA has a statutory power to make or amend the law in respect of money laundering. It is a long-established tenet of English law that delegated powers only extend to making an order under which acts committed abroad are only triable in the English courts if the power is confirmed in specific and unambiguous words in the applicable statute. Whether the provisions of the FSMA 2000 in respect of these delegated powers are, if challenged, deemed to be of sufficient clarity remains to be seen.

7.37   Part I of the CJA 1993 contains a list of substantive offences that are triable in England and Wales if any event to which the offence relates takes place within England or Wales, regardless of the location of the defendant at the time of that event taking place. For example, a deception committed in France by which funds are transferred from an account in the USA through a bank in London is deemed to be justiciable in England. The list of offences caught relates solely to property and conspiracy or attempts to commit property offences. The list is subdivided into two groups: in Group A are the substantive offences, and in Group B the inchoate[1]. The offences under Group A do not include investment offences such as insider dealing, but the general terminology of the FSMA, s 6 (financial crimes) includes deception and handling stolen goods, both of which are specifically mentioned under the CJA 1993.

1   Group A: theft, obtaining property by deception, obtaining a pecuniary advantage by deception, false accounting, false statements by company directors, procuring the execution of a valuable security by deception, blackmail, handling stolen goods, obtaining services by deception. Group B: conspiracy to commit a Group A offence, conspiracy to defraud, attempting/inciting another to commit a Group A offence. Also, conspiracy to defraud is an offence under s 12 of the CJA 1987, which preserves the common law offence, triable only on indictment (ten years' imprisonment and/or unlimited fine). In terms of international jurisdiction, a prosecution brought under the CJA 1993 has a significantly wider application.

7.38   Special provisions are made for offences that are committed against EU member states. Under the CJA 1997, s 71 it is an offence to be involved, within the UK, in the commission of a serious offence against a member state. This section does not seek to penalise offences committed elsewhere in the EU, it is solely restricted to those cases where a person assists or induces another in the commission of a serious offence, against a member state from within the UK[1]. The serious offences specified are principally related to fraud and evasion of fiscal liability. For the purposes of this section, a serious offence is one that can attract a custodial sentence of 12 months or more in the member state concerned. There appears to be no requirement to prove intention, but this may be open to challenge, as the penalty on conviction is up to seven years' imprisonment[2].

1 It follows that the inducer/assister cannot be convicted unless the other party has successfully committed the serious offence against the other member state. Evidence of the successful prosecution of the induced other party may be facilitated through the CJICA 1990.
2 CJA 1993, s 71(1); a challenge on the basis that the term of imprisonment is disproportional vis other strict liability offences and therefore it should be a requirement that the prosecution successfully discharge the burden of proof re intent.

7.39 The CJA 1993 has now brought together and clarified a number of former jurisdictional dilemmas. In the case of international transactions, jurisdiction may now rest in England and Wales in considerably more instances than prior to implementation of the CJA 1993[1]. In respect of those criminal matters likely to come to the attention of the FSA, mutual co-operation is facilitated through the FSMA 2000. What the CJA 1993 provides is a statutory framework for jurisdiction that is available to a number of investigation agencies including the FSA.

1 For example, the CJA 1993, s 5, as amended by the Criminal Attempts Act 1981, s 1(4), whereby previously an attempt could only be charged if the substantive offence was triable in England and Wales. The changes effectively opened the way for charging attempts made in this jurisdiction to commit substantive offences overseas irrespective of whether or not the substantive offence was justiciable here. Safeguards against abuse of this potential jurisdictional expansion have been brought about by ss 5–8 of the Criminal Justice (Terrorism and Conspiracy) Act 1998; it is now open to the defence to challenge the proposition that the alleged conduct is a criminal offence in the foreign state.

7.40 In August 1991 the UK ratified the European Convention on Mutual Assistance in Criminal Matters. Prior to this, arrangements for the service of process and facilitating cross-border assistance were largely informal and non-statutory. The ratification process was facilitated through the implementation of Part I of the CJICA 1990. The original provisions were limited in application, though, as they did not provide for the exchange of information relating to any fiscal investigations[1].

1 This has been remedied through the implementation of the Additional Protocol.

7.41 The CJICA 1990 enables the UK to co-operate with other countries in criminal investigations and proceedings, and it enables the UK to implement the Vienna Convention in respect of drugs trafficking and the seizure of drugs-related money. Section 1 of the CJICA 1990 deals with the service of overseas process in the UK. Under this section a country may apply to the Secretary of State to serve on a person who is in the UK, irrespective of his nationality, a summons or document issued by a court exercising criminal jurisdiction in that country. There is no requirement that the offence amounts to a criminal offence in the UK. There is no obligation on the recipient of the process to attend the overseas country, and there is no requirement on the UK to ensure that there is compliance[1].

1 CJICA 1990, s 1(3).

7.42 Section 2 of the CJICA 1990 deals with the service of UK process on persons overseas. This section provides that a summons or order may be served on a person whose attendance is sought at a UK court. It is not restricted to the service of criminal documents. In accordance with the principles of reciprocity, there is no requirement on the overseas country to ensure attendance, and there is also no penalty for non-attendance by the recipient[1].

1 Whereas, of course, it is an offence to fail to respond to a summons when you are domiciled in the UK: CJICA 1990, s 2(3).

7.43 The more interesting implications of the CJICA 1990 are contained within ss 3–4 and 7–9, which relate to the use of evidence obtained in one jurisdiction in the courts of another and the transfer of persons from one country to another for the purposes of criminal proceedings. Under s 3 a magistrate or judge may request assistance from an overseas authority on behalf of a UK prosecuting agency or the UK defendant. An application by the defendant may only be made once proceedings have been instituted. Requests from a potential defendant are not permissible[1]. The basis for a request by a prosecuting authority is unchallengeable, per se, but recourse through the provisions of the Human Rights Act 1998 would seem possible[2].

All applications should be made through a court and must be by the defence. They may be heard ex parte and in camera[3].

1 CJICA 1990, s 3(2).
2 On the basis that since there is no need for the requesting party to inform the other of a request for assistance, it follows that the fairness of any subsequent trial might be prejudiced.
3 Magistrates' Courts (Criminal Justice (International Co-operation)) Rules 1991, SI 1991/1074, r 6(1): 'An application under section 3 (1) of the Act (a) shall be heard in a petty-sessional court-house, (b) may be heard ex parte (2) ... direct that the public be excluded, (3) ... and without prejudice to any other powers of the court to hear proceedings in camera' (Crown Court Rules 1982, SI 1982/1109, r 31 (application for letters of request)). This has the same provisions as those available to the magistrate's court.

7.44 Any evidence obtained is restricted to use for the purposes specified in the letter of request. It would, for example, be inappropriate and contrary to the provisions for a party to seek to use overseas criminal evidence in civil debt recovery proceedings. This section is not as exclusive as it sounds though, for it is possible for an overseas country to permit use of the evidence for a purpose other than that specified in the letter[1].

1 CJICA 1990, s 3(7).

7.45 Once evidence has been obtained from an overseas country it must be presented before the UK courts in a manner that complies with domestic rules of evidence. Under the provisions of the Criminal Justice Act 1988[1] there are rules that permit the discretionary inclusion of documentary evidence. However, this may lead to unfairness at trial where the defendant does not have the opportunity to question the maker of the documentary testimony. The potential dilemma in respect of evidence obtained overseas is recognised and, under s 3(8) of the CJICA 1990, the UK court must have regard to[2]:

'(a) Whether it was possible to challenge the statement by questioning the person who made it; and (b) if proceedings have been instituted, to whether the local law allowed the parties to the proceedings to be legally represented when the evidence was being taken.'

1 See the CJICA 1990, ss 23 and 24 and the CJA 1998.
2 It is most likely that in such circumstances the FSA will adopt the approach taken by the Serious Fraud Office and the police, that is to send a member of the UK agency to the overseas country to attend the proceedings at which evidence is obtained. This may not prevent a successful challenge but will go some considerable way towards satisfying the UK courts that all reasonable steps were taken.

7.46 Section 4 of the CJICA 1990 has effect where the Secretary of State receives a request for assistance from an overseas country in connection with criminal proceedings that have been instituted, or a criminal investigation that is being carried on in that country. As in all cases, the Secretary of State has discretion in deciding whether to accommodate the request or not. The evidence sought must be relevant to the investigation or proceedings. On receipt of a request the Secretary of State will direct a court to receive the evidence, which may include more material than that which is ultimately presented at trial[1]. It has also been established that compliance with a request for discovery in the UK domestic courts will not be prevented on the basis that to do so would amount to a criminal offence in another jurisdiction[2]. If an overseas request is one related to serious fraud, the Secretary of State may refer the request to the Director of the Serious Fraud Office for him to obtain the evidence requested[3].

1 The employment of the term 'evidence' appears to have wider use than 'admissible evidence' at the overseas trial. It has been held that information that may lead to the discovery of evidence is included within the scope of evidence that may be obtained by the UK for an overseas investigation: *R v Secretary of State for the Home Department, ex p Fininvest SpA* [1997] 1 All ER 942, [1997] 1 WLR 743; and see Kirk, D and Woodcock, *A Serious Fraud: Investigation and Trial* (1997, 2nd edn), p 325.
2 See *Partenreederei v Grosvenor Grain and Feed Co Ltd* [1993] 2 Lloyd's Rep 324, where two French defendants unsuccessfully sought to have an order for discovery of documents discharged on the basis that compliance would amount to a criminal offence in France. Mr Justice Cresswell held that (1) the court was not persuaded that any criminal offence would be committed by the defendants if they complied with the order for discovery in the English action; (2) neither party had found any English decision where it had been found that the court should not order discovery against a French party: and French companies in the past had regularly given discovery in legal proceedings in England without prosecution; and (3) a defendant who has given notice of intention to defend has to abide by local laws.

3 The CJOC 1990, s 4 as amended by s 164 of the Criminal Justice and Public Order Act 1994, which inserts sub-s (2A), the proviso relating to the Director of the SFO, after s 4 (2) (a), (b). The provisions of the Criminal Justice Act 1987 were also amended accordingly (under the CJA 1987, s 1 (a), (b) inserted by s 1A) to facilitate the extended powers of the Director of the SFO. These provisions came into force in February 1995.

7.47 Challenges to the jurisdiction of local courts are particularly prevalent in international financial crime cases, as the challenge itself is a delaying tactic and increases all parties' costs. Complex multi-national frauds invariably raise issues of applicable law when the investigators are seeking to obtain evidence from another jurisdiction. The obtaining of the evidence is rarely in itself contentious; it is the subsequent use of that evidence which may give grounds for challenge. When a financial crime is perpetrated by company officials, the opportunity to delay the inquiry by applications for judicial review are a legitimate and effective means of causing the substantive proceedings to remain dormant. Questions of foreign law are questions of fact, which must be proved to requisite applicable standard. It follows that 'There is no shortage of opportunity for the well advised defendant to raise legitimate challenges to the jurisdiction of the English courts'[1].

1 Friedman, P 'Jurisdiction and Beyond', *New Law Journal* (4 August 1995), p 1159.

7.48 The CJICA 1990, s 7 deals with additional co-operation powers. Under this section police officers[1] have authority to search for and seize materials on behalf of an overseas authority. The procedure for such assistance is the same as elsewhere under the Act. The requesting overseas state must make an application via the Secretary of State. The evidence sought must relate to an offence that equates to a serious arrestable offence for the purposes of the relevant UK law. Once directed by the Secretary of State, a police officer may apply to a magistrate for a warrant to enter, by force if necessary, and to search for and to seize any evidence. This provision does not extend to arrest. If a summary power of arrest is exercised in relation to an overseas investigation it will not attract the same power to search that exists under the provisions of the Police and Criminal Evidence Act 1984. Searches conducted under these circumstances would be unlawful[2].

1 CJICA 1990, s 7(7): the Secretary of State may by order direct that any of those powers shall also be exercisable by a person of any other description specified in the order, eg appointed FSA investigators.
2 CJICA 1990, s 8 deals with comparable provisions for the execution of warrants in Scotland.

7.49 Under the CJICA 1990, s 9 there is a power to enforce overseas forfeiture orders in the UK. The measures relate to offences of drugs trafficking, and any other criminal offence which corresponds to or is similar to an indictable offence in the UK. Under this section a court may order the forfeiture and destruction or forfeiture and disposal of anything which was used in connection with the commission of the offence[1].

1 The confiscation provisions relate to offences contained within Pt VI of the Criminal Justice Act 1988 as amended by the Proceeds of Crime Act 1995 (which came into force on

1 November 1995). Offences of a relevant description are: drugs trafficking; offences relating to clubs, gaming and sex establishments under the Criminal Justice Act 1988, Sch 4; any other indictable offence and offences under the Prevention of Terrorism Act (Temporary Provisions) Act 1989, as amended.

7.50   The CJICA 1990 goes beyond the requirements of the European Convention on Mutual Assistance and extends the possibility of mutual co-operation to any country. Assistance is discretionary in most cases, but the expectation is that the UK will always co-operate with Convention state requests.

European directives, conventions and mutual assistance

7.51   As seen above, the Commission or Council of the EU can require member states' regulators to take action to deprive non-EEA firms access to the EEA financial markets. The authority to invoke this reciprocal action derives from EC directives. The four directives concerned, the Investment Services Directive (93/22/EEC), the Credit Institutions Directive (2000/12/EC), the First Life Insurance Directive (79/267/EEC) and the Non-Life Insurance Directive (73/239/EEC), are specific in the requirements that are placed on the domestic recipient states; for example, art 9(1) of the Investment Services Directive states:

> 'Member states shall require any person who proposes to acquire, directly or indirectly, a qualifying holding in an investment firm first to inform the competent authorities, telling them the size of the intended holding.'

7.52   It was the intention of the Commission that there would be a total freedom of capital movement within the EEA. This was perhaps rather ambitious given the fragmented developmental stages of the various financial markets within the EEA; nevertheless a system of passporting has been established whereby the host state will assume responsibility for supervision of the non-domestic firm. The Investment Services Directive is silent on the issue of cross-border assistance between regulators, and this has resulted in each member State developing the necessary measures that go beyond the requirements of the Directives[1] through domestic legislation. In real terms this is unlikely to prevent effective regulation as both the Investment Services Directive and the FSMA 2000 incorporate the requirement that the home state has a complete record of the passported firms' activities and that these are available on request to the host state regulator[2], with the proviso that confidentiality is respected[3].

1   For example, the control provisions relating to all UK authorised persons (FSMA 2000, s 178(4)) goes beyond the requirements under the Investment Services Directive.
2   Investment Services Directive, art 20. In addition, art 23(3) of the Directive requires each regulator to collaborate closely with the relevant other member state regulator.
3   Investment Services Directive, art 25.

7.53   General mutual assistance measures have continued to be the subject of discussion since the original Council of Europe Convention[1]. The 1959 Convention applied to all criminal offences except fiscal, military or political[2]. Article 1 states that:

> 'The contracting parties undertake to afford each other, in accordance with the provisions of this Convention, the widest measure of mutual assistance in proceedings in respect of offences, the punishment of which, at the time of the request for assistance, falls within the jurisdiction of the judicial authorities of the requesting Parties.'

The 1978 Protocol[3] removed the exemption relating to fiscal matters.

1   The European Convention on Mutual Assistance in Criminal Matters 1959.
2   Opened for signature 20/04/59; signed by the UK 21/06/91; ratified 29/08/91; in force 27/11/91.
3   Ratified by all member states except Belgium and Luxembourg. Signed by the UK 21/06/91 and in force 27/11/91.

7.54   A new Convention was introduced in May 2000 to 'improve the speed and efficiency of judicial co-operation'[1] and to 'encourage and modernise co-operation between judicial, police and customs authorities'[2], in particular in the area of combating organised crime, laundering the proceeds of crime[3] and financial crime[4].

1   Judicial Co-operation in Criminal Matters, OJ C 197, 12 July 2000, Council Act 29 May 2000, 1) Objective. Available at europa.eu.int/scadplus/leg.
2   Judicial Co-operation in Criminal Matters, OJ C 197, 12 July 2000, Council Act 29 May 2000, 3) Contents. Available at europa.eu.int/scadplus/leg.
3   This does not alter the status of the Convention on Laundering, Search, Seizure and Confiscation of the Proceeds of Crime. Opened for signature 08/11/90; signed by UK 08/11/90; in force 01/09/93.
4   Insider dealing is contained within the Convention on Insider Trading Directive 89/592, OJ 1989 L334/30; opened for signature 20/04/89; signed by UK 13/09/89; in force 01/10/91; and the additional Protocol to the Convention on Insider Trading, signed 13/09/89 and in force 01/10/91. Related Conventions include the Convention on Protection of Financial Interests (Fraud Convention) OJ 1995 C 316/48 and Convention on Corruption OJ 1997 C 195/1 (with Explanatory Report, OJ 1998 C 391/1).

7.55   The 2000 Convention significantly increases the authority to assist member states and the previous requirement that all requests go through a central authority has been removed[1], and as a general rule communications may now be made directly between judicial authorities with territorial competence[2]. In certain cases it is still necessary to go through the previously established formal channels, for example where the transit of a person held in custody is concerned. Urgent requests may still be made through Interpol.

1   This Convention also proposes, at art 18(4), that future Conventions can become active on ratification by only two member states, ie that the two states concerned could agree to implement all of the provisions between themselves without further recourse to other states. The real effect of this is domestic, however, as in practice it would prevent parliament from obstructing the implementation of a Convention once it has been signed by government.
2   2000 Convention, art 4.

7.56 A judicial authority or central authority may make direct contact with an investigation authority in another member state. The recipient state may choose to accept or refuse to apply this clause. A refusal does not prevent the requesting state making a fresh application through formal channels. A spontaneous exchange of information, without any prior request, may take place between member states regarding criminal offences and administrative infringements, the punishment or handling of which falls within the competence of the receiving authority[1]. It can be seen that what started in 1959 as a fairly modest attempt to facilitate mutual co-operation has now, under the 2000 provisions, developed into a series of complex measures with considerable beneficial scope as well as implications for the fundamental rights of cross-jurisdiction suspects in financial investigations.

1   2000 Convention, art 6.

7.57 The 2000 Convention increases the specific forms of assistance that may be provided. If stolen objects are found in another member state, ordinarily they would be returned to the home state. In certain circumstances the requested state may refrain from returning the goods if in doing so it would facilitate the restitution of the articles to the rightful owner[1].

1   2000 Convention, art 7.

7.58 A person held in a member state that has requested an investigation be conducted in another member state may be temporarily transferred to the investigating state[1]. Two or more member states may set up a joint investigation team, the composition of which is to be set out in a joint agreement between the member states concerned. This extends to covert operations that may be conducted by officers acting under covert or false identity, provided the national law and procedures of the member state where the investigation is conducted are complied with. Earth satellite communications interception may take place on the territory of the a member state without the authority of that state if no technical assistance is needed from the state where the action is to take place[2].

1   Subject to the consent of the person held in the requesting state: 2000 Convention, art 8.
2   2000 Convention, arts 10 and 11. It is difficult to accept that these measures have been sufficiently thought through given, inter alia, the potential problems that may be encountered in respect of jurisdiction, powers to arrest, interview, carry firearms, to have access to legal representation, and defendant rights to cross-examine witnesses, etc, as well as the differing member state provisions relating to data protection and privacy. The position is little better for the cross-border witness who is subject to local perjury laws; there is no right to an interpreter or counsel. It would appear that these articles may represent future fertile territory for human rights challenges.

7.59 Any personal data obtained may only be used by the obtaining state for:

• judicial or administrative proceedings covered by the Convention;
• preventing an immediate and serious threat to public security; and
• for any other purpose, with the prior consent of the communicating member state or the data subject[1].

S Peers states, in *EU Justice and Home Affairs Law*[2]:

'Clearly, all of these measures will allow the prosecuting state to assert its authority de facto over persons and evidence in another member state, albeit through the de jure veil of acts of the other member state's authorities.'

1   2000 Convention, art 14. NB for 'any other purpose' is with prior consent of the member state *or* the data subject. Special provisions do apply to the non-Schengen states, and to Luxembourg, Norway and Iceland.
2   Peers, S EU Justice and Home Affairs Law (2000), p 171.

7.60   France has proposed an initiative to the effect that member states will encourage the provision and securing of documents, information and other data likely to constitute evidence of money laundering[1]:

'At the request of another member state, each member state is required to provide the bank account numbers of persons being prosecuted or under suspicion in the requesting member state. If the request for mutual legal assistance relates to the serious form of organised crime or money laundering, the member state which receives the request for mutual assistance must also provide details of banking operations carried out by those persons, except where the request is likely to jeopardise the essential interests of the member state.'

1   Official Journal No C 243, 24 August 2000.

7.61   On 19 July 2000 Portugal, France, Sweden and Belgium presented two initiatives with a view to:

- adopting a Council Decision setting up Eurojust with a view to reinforcing the fight against serious organised crime; and
- adopting a Decision setting up a Provisional Judicial Co-operation Unit.

7.62   In response to the demands of the single currency, the globalisation of financial markets and new trends in electronic trading, the efficacy of EU mutual assistance provision in the financial service sector is reviewed by the Financial Services Policy Group. The Group was created at the request of the Vienna European Council in 1998 with a view to imparting strategic vision to EU-level action in respect of financial markets.

7.63   At its third meeting in March 1999, the Group addressed whether the infrastructure for supervision of the financial service sector was meeting the multiplicity of demands created by an increasingly integrated market. It was felt, as a matter of urgency, that a series of measures needed to be taken to remove obstacles that prevented a pan-European securities and derivatives market. To this end, there was strong support for a review of the Investment Services Directive, legislation to prevent and deter market manipulation, and coherent implementation of the Settlement Finality Directive. The Group noted that present arrangements for bi-lateral co-operation worked well but may not be sufficient in view of the restructuring of the European financial sector, and the emphasis should be placed on greater cross-sectoral co-operation and co-ordination as the basis for future developments. It was also suggested that continued consideration be given to the creation of a single authority to enforce any future integrated market rules[1]:

'There has been a strong call for a clear and coherent EU voice and input in the shaping and activities of nascent new structures for international supervisory co-operation. The EU has long stressed the importance of common prudential norms and enforcement infrastructure as part of the panacea for international financial turmoil. By virtue of its track record in regulating and managing prudential risk, the EU has a significant contribution to make in this context. The Commission will continue efforts to make sure that a common EU view can be presented[2].'

1   It may transpire that if greater integration of international markets occurs there will be a need for a global regulator. In the event of this happening a number of markets may look towards Europe for a model given the current, and proposed, volume of integration and 'passporting' that exists. Further comments on this point will be made in the conclusion to this chapter.
2   Financial Services Policy Group, third meeting. Available at europa.eu.int/comm/ internal_market.

7.64   Since this meeting the Financial Services Policy Group has considered, and supports, the proposal contained within the Amsterdam Treaty[1] to give effect to a fast-track procedure for financial services legislation[2]. This support has now been the subject of further progress in the financial services priorities of the Commission[3] where, inter alia, the Commission is preparing a new proposal for market information which could simplify 'shelf registration' techniques for companies that wish to have their shares publicly traded[4], and it is preparing a Directive on collateral to facilitate cross-border collateralisation techniques and, in doing so, to reduce the current degree of legal uncertainty that exists. The Financial Services Action Plan also stressed the importance of mutual co-operation between regulators, and the Commission has committed itself to making new legislation to tackle the prudential issues raised by mixed financial conglomerates[5].

1   Amsterdam Treaty, art 251.
2   Conclusions of the Financial Services Policy Group, 19/10/99. Available at europa.eu.int/comm/internal_market.
3   As outlined in the Commission Report on the Financial Services Action Plan, 31 May 2000. Available at MARKT-C1@cec.eu.int.
4   In recognition of the fact that multiple listings and cross-border share offers are rare and the existing legislation, requiring that the partner country markets the same information as domestic authorities, has been ineffective.
5   In addition the Council and European Parliament have adopted the E-Money Directive and a Directive amending the insurance directives and the Investment Services Directive. It will soon be permissible for member states to exchange information with third countries. There are new Directives on market manipulation and the Commission and European Central Bank have suggested the abolition of reporting requirements of banks in respect of cross-border payments for monetary policy purposes. The Committee of Wise Men chaired

by Baron Lamfalussy (set up at 17 July 2000 ECOFIN Council) has added support to these proposals within its remit to ensure greater convergence and co-operation in day to day synthesis of developments in the securities markets.

7.65   On 21 August 2000 the FSA issued a joint statement with the German regulatory authorities relating to the proposal that would merge the Deutsche Börse AG and the London Stock Exchange into a joint group iX-international exchanges plc. The announcement stated that[1]:

'The authorities emphasise in this paper that the development of iX-international exchanges plc needs to take full account of requirements of market integrity – in particular the prevention of insider dealing and market abuse – and of market transparency and the protection of investors.'

Dealing specifically with the issue of financial crimes, the FSA and German authorities agreed to ensure that co-ordinated and effective enforcement action be taken, and in those cases where there is a common interest the authorities would act together to consider the impact that the offending action might have on either or both markets. The communiqué stated that: 'Experience gained at FESCO level will be particularly helpful for developing practical arrangements'[2].

1   Joint Statement by the UK and German supervisory authorities on regulatory issues concerning iX-international exchanges plc, FSA/PN/111/2000. Available at fsa.gov.uk/pubs/press.
2   Joint Statement by the UK and German supervisory authorities on regulatory issues concerning iX-international exchanges plc, FSA/PN/111/2000. Available at fsa.gov.uk/pubs/press.

The Forum of European Securities Commissions

7.66   FESCO was founded to facilitate the creation of a single market in financial services. Membership comprises 17 EEA statutory securities commissions[1]. The principal activity of FESCO is to develop common regulatory standards within the framework of existing EC law or to provide direction on appropriate standards in the event of no relevant law being in place.

1   The 15 EU Member States, plus Norway and Iceland.

7.67   Implementation of FESCO standards is ensured as each member state is responsible for application in its domestic jurisdiction. Current areas of FESCO activity are the harmonisation of disclosure rules for companies and greater protection of investors from fraud and financial crimes committed by firms. In the absence of relevant binding legislation, FESCO utilises Multilateral Memoranda of Understanding as a means of facilitating change quickly and efficiently if market integrity is compromised. For example, the FESCO Multilateral Memorandum on the Exchange of Information of securities activities caused the creation of FESCOPOL whose purpose is 'To facilitate effective, efficient and pro-active sharing of information, in order to enhance the co-operation and the co-ordination of surveillance and enforcement activities between FESCO members'[1]. Soon after its creation, FESCOPOL presented a Multilateral Memorandum of Understanding to 'create a pan-European regulatory framework to provide the broadest possible mutual assistance between the competent authorities of member states of EEA so as to enhance market surveillance and effective enforcement against financial crime'[2]. The scope of the Memorandum of Understanding covers investigations into insider dealing, market manipulation and financial frauds, and investigations into and the monitoring of compliance. The Memorandum is open for non-EEA states to sign[3]:

> 'It would be wrong to name FESCO as the Euro-SEC as it is not yet fully established and has yet to work out formal procedures ... However, in terms of the contribution it will make to regulatory co-operation between EEA states, it seems likely that it is currently the vehicle which can best ensure the European financial services markets remain transparent and fair ....'

1   See 'FESCOPOL's Presentation' at www.europefesco.org.
2   See 'FESCOPOL's Presentation' at www.europefesco.org.
3   Watson, J, 'International Co-Operation in the Field of Financial Regulatory Enforcement', Part 2 – The EU Approach, *Butterworths Journal of International Banking and Financial Law*, vol 15, No 1, January 2000, pp 13–16 at p 15.

International obligations

7.68   The specific international obligations introduced in the FSMA 2000, s 410 are of some interest due to the considerable latitude it gives the Treasury to direct UK regulators[1] to modify a proposed course of action if that action were to be incompatible with any Community or international obligations. This provision represents one of only two examples within the FSMA 2000 where the Treasury has an absolute authority to override the actions of the FSA[2].

1   The FSA, the FSA as Listing Authority, RCHs and RIEs (other than overseas), any person included in the list under the FSMA 2000, s 301, and the Ombudsman Company acting under Pt XVI of the Act.
2   The other example is in respect of competition matters.

7.69   Before discussing the range of informal agreements that exist to facilitate the exchange of information between regulators, two further pieces of legislation warrant commentary. The extradition of subjects between nation states has been formally recognised in the UK since 1870, which saw the first of a number of Acts that facilitate the return of fugitive offenders to a requesting state. More recent legislation, the Extradition Act 1989, has moved away from the principle that in all circumstances the requesting state must establish a prima facia case, and further changes have been brought about in respect of exchanges relating to less serious offences, under the

Criminal Justice and Public Order Act 1994[1]. Under the parent Act (the Extradition Act 1989) orders in council were made to the effect that the UK has formal extradition agreements with the commonwealth countries, all signatories to the European Convention and a number of other states listed in the 1994 Order. Further supplementary provisions provide that extradition shall take place between EU states if the offences correspond to an offence that exists in the requested state[2]. If a request is received in the UK for the arrest of an overseas fugitive, and the offence alleged is theft or handling stolen goods, the court that issues the arrest warrant may also add the provision that a search may be made of the premises where the arrested person is detained. What amounts to an extradition offence is not specified, but it will include financial crimes, Inland Revenue offences, insider dealing[3] and conspiracy to defraud[4]. Challenges to the status of the alleged crime are made before the magistrate's court, where the suspect may submit that the extradition offence does not amount to a serious crime in either country[5].

1   Criminal Justice and Public Order Act 1994, s 158(5)(b) has implications in respect of proceedings at summary trial.
2   European Convention on Extradition (Fiscal Offences) Order 1993, SI 1993/2663.
3   Specifically added by virtue of Sch 1 of the Criminal Justice Act 1988.
4   These should be viewed in the context of Pt 1 of the CJA 1993 to the extent that jurisdiction over matters to be heard in this country are considerably extended by the 1993 Act.
5   Appeals against the decision of the magistrate's court are by way of case stated.

7.70   The Regulation of Investigatory Powers Act 2000 ('RIPO 2000') ostensibly deals with the interception of communications by UK investigating authorities. There are also provisions under the Act to give full accord to mutual assistance requests. It follows that a warrant may be issued to authorise a UK investigation agency to intercept communications on behalf of an overseas authority. Application for an interception warrant must be through a senior officer of the relevant authority, which includes a person who, for the purposes of any international mutual assistance agreement, is the competent authority of a country or territory outside the UK[1]. Ordinarily all warrants are scrutinised and issued by the Secretary of State, and this authority may not be designated; however, in respect of overseas requests made under an international mutual assistance agreement[2] a warrant may be issued by a senior official[3].

1   RIPO 2000, s 6(2)(j).
2   Defined in the RIPO 2000, s 1(4)(a), (b), (c).
3   RIPO 2000, s 7 (2)(b).

7.71   The term 'communication' applies to telephone numbers, e-mail accounts and all other forms of telecommunication; it does not apply, inter alia, to postal items for the purposes of this part of the RIPO 2000. The communications to be intercepted must be identified; these might include communications from, or intended for, the person specified in the warrant, or transmissions to, or from, specified premises[1]. A warrant will cease to have effect at the end of the relevant period unless it is renewed.

1   RIPO 2000, s 8(2), (3).

7.72   As well as authorising the interception of telecommunications, the Secretary of State may authorise intrusive surveillance and covert intelligence gathering. Applications for authorisation will normally be from the intelligence services and the Ministry of Defence, but it is also permissible for applications to be made from other designated public authorities[1].

1   RIPO 2000, s 41(1)(d).

7.73   Where an offence under any of the provisions of the RIPO 2000[1] is committed by a body corporate, and the consent, connivance or negligence of the director, manager, secretary or similar officer is proven, he, as well as the body corporate, shall be guilty of that offence[2]. Criminal conduct for the purpose of the RIPO 2000 includes conduct that results in substantial financial gain or conduct by a large number of persons in pursuit of a common purpose[3].

1   Other than Pt III matters (Investigation of Electronic Data protected by Encryption).
2   RIPO 2000, s 79 (1)(a), (b).
3   RIPO 2000, s 81 (2)(a), (b) and (3)(a), (b).

7.74   Statutory provisions do not represent the only channel through which international assistance initiatives are established, and a common feature of regulatory co-operation is the Memoranda of Understanding ('MOU'). These can be multilateral or bi-lateral; they are not legally binding and they only apply to the voluntary signatories to the agreement. The principle underlying the MOU is that signatories will afford each other the fullest level of mutual assistance possible[1], the only significant restriction being that each party must respect any domestic restrictions relating to legal confidentiality. Perhaps not surprisingly, examples of the most effective MOUs are with those countries with whom the UK has the more sophisticated political and economic relationships – for example the USA.

1   Eg, questioning suspects, obtaining documents, conducting reciprocal compliance inspections and participating in investigations.

7.75   An MOU has been defined as[1]:

'Statements of intent which do not impose legally binding obligations on signatories. As such, they have no power to overcome domestic laws and regulations, nor do they affect other channels of co-operation, such as mutual assistance in criminal matters. The strength of MOU's, however, is that they facilitate the exchange of information by accommodating the differences between regulators and by responding to changing legal environments.'

1   Principles of Memoranda of Understanding, The Report of the Working Party No 4. Available at www.iosco.org/principles_ of_ memoranda-document.

7.76   The MOU is essentially a vehicle for the exchange of information and the provision of assistance. The degree of formality attached to it is a variable, and the spectrum typically ranges from letters of agreement between individual regulators to more formal instruments between entire agencies. It is important to appreciate, however, that the MOU does not represent a legal agreement between countries, albeit it may be the precursor to a subsequent Treaty.

The International Organisation of Securities Commissions

7.77   The nature of financial crimes is such that jurisdictional issues may well be multi-national rather than bi-lateral. As a consequence of this, a number of regulators have been persuaded to establish contact groups and develop multi-lateral agreements.

7.78   IOSCO was established in 1983. There are currently 135 member agencies that have resolved to:

- co-operate together to ensure a better regulation of the markets;
- exchange information on their respective experiences;
- unite their efforts to establish standards and effective surveillance; and
- promote mutual assistance by a rigorous application of the standards.

7.79   IOSCO does not operate on the basis of a constitutional treaty but through the informal application of byelaws. Binding resolutions are passed, by majority vote, at its annual conferences. In 1994 the Committee passed a Mutual Assistance and Co-operation resolution to commit members to examine their own laws and, by doing so, to evaluate their own ability to facilitate and progress co-operation with overseas regulators. It was recognised that those members who came from the less sophisticated financial markets might be disadvantaged in preventing financial crimes due to lack of regulatory experience and financial resources. Consequently, all members are called upon to provide assistance on a reciprocal basis and to consider the implementation of bi-lateral agreements as a vehicle for the effective enablement of assistance. To assist members further, the Technical Committee produced the Principles for Memoranda of Understanding[1] that identifies the specific components necessary for an effective MOU[2].

1   Presented on September 1991.
2   The subject headings are: Subject Matter, Confidentiality, Implementation Procedures, The Rights of Persons Subject to an MOU Request, Consultation, Public Policy Exception, Types of Assistance, Participation by the Requesting Authority and Cost-Sharing.

7.80   Interestingly, the Principles for Memorandum of Understanding specify that, in the event of an assisting authority being unable to facilitate a request due to the restrictions of its domestic laws, that member regulator should seek to recommend measures to rectify the domestic legislation. On this point the Principles state that[1]:

'The ability to compel production of documents and statements or testimony on behalf of a foreign authority greatly enhances the value of MOUs. Authorities that do not have such an ability should take all reasonable steps ... to remove impediments that keep them from utilising their full domestic powers for providing assistance to foreign authorities.'

1   Principles for Memorandum of Understanding: 7 Types of Assistance.

7.81   Through the auspices of IOSCO, the FSA has entered into 26 MOUs concerning the exchange of information between itself and foreign countries and territories[1].

1   A number of these involve other UK agencies and departments, eg the DTI, HM Treasury and the London Stock Exchange (as effective from 10 August 2000). Details available at www.iosco.org/mou-united_kingdom.

7.82   IOSCO has been through a number of changes since its inception, but overall it appears to have contributed significantly in progressing effective international regulatory compliance and dilution of circumvention through regulatory arbitrage.

Regulatory assistance: a future perspective

7.83   The unitary national regulator is now established. There is support for this model to be enlarged towards a transnational or global regulator. The impetus for single global regulation will be influenced by a number of factors, inter alia, questions of enforcement viability and effectiveness, the impact of global or transnational regulation on individual sectors of the financial markets and the implications of international financial competitiveness from the national perspective. There will also be the issue of national and international rules and the compatibility of laws and the question of whether global is all encompassing and, if not, what measures will be available to restrict the transference of business onto the errant jurisdictions which permit less stringent compliance. As we have seen, creating effective rules is complex. The rule-making process is structured by reference to national, EC and international demands. The process is informed by political and organisational pressures that operate within the financial markets. The result is that there is frequently compromise and pragmatism with an element of trade-off between desired and workable objectives.

7.84   At one extreme, it is perhaps impossible to imagine that there could be an effective global regulator; conversely, the notion of a unitary domestic regulator may have seemed impractical and unlikely in the past. The reality is that now most market participants would accept the merits of a single regulator for one-stop compliance assistance, enforcement and consumer protection. Although the process of regulation is unlikely to result in a televised serial along the lines of 'NYPD Blue' or 'The Bill', it is a most effective way of deterring miscreant practices by individuals and corporations who operate within financial markets.

7.85 In future it can be anticipated that regulation will be the pre-eminent method employed to encourage, educate and control increasingly sophisticated domestic and international financial provision. Regulation is cost-effective as a criminal trial is frequently the last resort. If matters do result in a criminal prosecution, a number of offences that are captured are strict liability and therefore do not require prosecutorial proof of intent; in addition the burden of proof has been significantly shifted towards the defendant in a number of cases. Regulation is attractive to governments as it creates the impression of delegating responsibility to market participants and reverts costs back onto the industry rather than the public purse. If the stigma of criminal liability is sought in cases where it is felt that an example needs to be made, then this can be accommodated through the imposition of criminal sanctions.

7.86 Regulatory offences have now increased in volume and sophistication; they have proliferated in appearance on statutes and they have been endorsed in the courts. Regulatory offences may lack the 'glamour of crimes', but they are effective[1]. Regulation is here to stay.

1   The use of the term 'glamour of crimes' in this context refers to Webb, K *Controlling Corporate Misconduct through Regulatory Offences: The Canadian Experience; Corporate Crime: Contemporary Debates* (Pearce, F and Snider, L eds) (1996), pp 339–351. Webb explains that 'The reader may quite justifiably wonder what is glamorous about crimes. The best way to explain this is by referring to a debate over regulatory offences versus crimes in which the author was involved, where I noted: "I must admit, though, I'm at a psychological disadvantage, in trying to persuade you of the strengths of regulatory offences. The trouble is, when compared with the word 'crimes' the phrase 'regulatory offences' strikes fear in the hearts of no one. Imagine the blasé response of the literary world if Dostoyevsky had entitled his book Regulatory Offences and Compliance instead of Crime and Punishment".'

7.87 On 17 May 2000 Michel Prada[1] stated that:

'Liberalisation of markets and globalisation, which exploded from about the mid 1980's, placed the regulators of many countries, and particularly those of Western Europe, in the position of having to accept modifications to their rules and introduce innovations which would put issuers and markets in a position where they could confront competition and avoid relocation. In reality the regulators themselves are in competition[2].'

If this view is accepted in part, if not in whole, then the arguments in favour of global regulation increase significantly as standardisation would engender harmony between regulators.

1   Chairman of Commission des Opérations de Bourse, France, Paper entitled 'Plenary 1, Global markets, Global Regulation', presented at the 25th IOSCO Annual Conference, Sydney, Australia.

2   Chairman of Commission des Opérations de Bourse, France, Paper entitled 'Plenary 1, Global markets, Global Regulation', presented at the 25th IOSCO Annual Conference, Sydney, Australia.

7.88   There is a precedent for attempted standardisation: the creation of FESCO. As seen above, a number of logistical hurdles have caused delay in the implementation of key objectives, and this may prove to be a key factor in preventing the globalisation that attracts the support of IOSCO.

7.89   The move towards a single market in financial services within the EU does not necessarily mean a move towards a single regulator. The strategic objectives of the Commission are to:

- establish a single market in wholesale financial services;
- make retail markets safe and secure; and
- strengthen the rules on prudential supervision.

7.90   However, it is difficult to envisage an integrated market without a commonality of terms and procedures, which extends to rules and laws. The continued development of a cross-border securities and derivatives market necessitates a common body of regulatory objectives and a method for its implementation. Without legal and operational certainty, the development of trans-European financial services is likely to be little more than rhetoric.

7.91   A single Euro-Regulator would be advantageous from a number of perspectives; the current plethora of administrative, public and private laws could be simplified and harmonised within a framework of single market rules providing a range of clear and transparent information for consumers throughout the EU and EEA member states. Matters for redress could be dealt with within the nation state of the aggrieved party. Settlements could be negotiated through one set of rules and an agreed cross-state implementation strategy[1]. The overall impact of such a move would be to reinforce consumer confidence and promote the Commission objective of securing further market integration[2]. These are ambitious plans and are unlikely to progress unchallenged by a number of individual financial market providers. What is more likely in the short term is increased collaboration between markets that fall short of total European harmonisation.

1   This has, to some extent, been progressed through the launching of FIN-NET. This is a Commission initiative that groups together 35 financial provision mediation bodies to facilitate out of court settlements in matters of consumer disputes. The blueprint of FIN-NET, promotion of consumer confidence through simple, rapid and inexpensive alternatives to traditional dispute resolution number of features that are transposable to a broader arena within a unified EU financial market.
2   This measure has progressed in part with the proposed creation of an EU Securities Advisory Committee. Any disparities that exist between member states on rules appertaining to Corporate Governance are considered at present to be unclear and therefore it is felt that any Community initiative in this area should be confined to reviewing national codes rather than seeking to introduce Eurowide provisions. See further 'Implementing the framework for financial markets: action plan', available at europa.eu.int/scadplus/leg/en.

7.92 Support for a European Securities Commission has come from a number of quarters and is predominantly based on the premise that a single market needs a single regulator. It has been argued that the barrier to effective harmonisation has been largely due to the disparity that exists between the legal systems. This does not, however, satisfactorily address the supposition that effective regulation is not a precursor to prosecution but an entity in itself that can transcend national legal barriers.

7.93 The only current example of a Euro-wide regulator is the European Central Bank, which of course has regulatory jurisdiction over single currency matters but not the securities markets. On one hand it can be said that to continue with 28 separate national stock exchanges' and 15 regulatory authorities is tantamount to supporting institutionalised chaos; conversely, to suggest that it is possible to harmonise 15 authorities is impractical and a recipe for federalised confusion. Whether domestic regulatory monopolies survive is outside of the parameters of this work, but reference to the American model, the Securities Exchange Commission ('SEC'), suggests that a federal model is advantageous and commands considerable respect amongst global financial institutions. It has been forcefully argued[1] that, prior to the US crash of 1932, which led to the creation of SEC, a number of commentators posited the value of a federal regulator. However, it was not until after the crash that residue reluctance diminished and the merits of a single authority were universally recognised. It is the view of some commentators[2] that there is no need for Europe to repeat the mistakes of the USA; rathermore, it can learn from them and create a federal regulator now.

1   For an informative discussion on the merits of a European Securities Commission see Thieffry, G 'Towards a European Securities Commission', *International Financial Law Review* (1999), Vol 18, No 9, pp 14–18.
2   See Thieffry, G 'Towards a European Securities Commission', *International Financial Law Review* (1999), Vol 18, No 9, pp 14–18.

7.94 As far back as 1998, the Finance Ministers and Central Bank Governors of G7 commissioned a report into the viability of enhanced co-operation between international financial markets. The Tietmeyer report[1] proposed the setting up of a Financial Stability Forum comprising[2]:

' ... national authorities responsible for financial stability in significant international financial centres, sector-specific international groupings of regulators, international financial institutions charged with surveillance of domestic and international financial systems and committees of central bank experts concerned with market infrastructure and functioning.'

The Financial Stability Forum was established in April 1999 under the chairmanship of Andrew Crockett, General Manager of the Bank of International Settlements. Membership has now extended to Australia, Hong Kong, Singapore and The Netherlands[3].

1 Hans Tietmeyer, President of Deutsche Bundesbank, presented his report, 'International Co-operation and Co-ordination in the Area of Financial Market Supervision and Surveillance', at the G7 Ministers and Governors meeting in Bonn, 20 February 1999.
2 See further 'Implementing the framework for financial markets: action plan', available at europa.eu.int/scadplus.
3 Current issues of Financial Stability Forum activity include consideration of measures to reduce the volatility of capital flows and the risk of short-term indebtedness and the impact on financial stability of off-shore financial centres.

7.95 Perhaps not surprisingly, the Tietmeyer Report is complementary to a number of existing measures and it pays due accord to a wide range of established international Committees that have contributed towards raising the standard and effectiveness of risk prevention on a global basis. It also supports the development of greater harmonisation and adds considerable weight to the pro-globalised regulation debate, even if the support is couched in fairly diffuse terms at times. In essence, the Financial Stability Forum supports concerted compliance procedures to combat systemic risk, international rules and standards of best practice and improved arrangements for the continuous flow of information between authorities responsible for regulation and compliance[1].

1 'Advances on issues such as consistent rules for the treatment of risk, arrangements for the pooling of information, and closer co-operation between the different supervisory authorities continue to be hampered by the fact that countries have different financial and supervisory systems', International Co-operation and Co-ordination in the Area of Financial Market Supervision and Surveillance, report by Hans Tietmeyer, 11 February 1999. Available at www.fsforum.org/About/TietmPaper.

7.96 The rationale for the establishment of the FSA is equally convincing as a rationale for the implementation of a global regulator, albeit that this is unlikely to receive the support of the FSA or HM government[1].

1 On the basis that the financial and legislative investment in the creation of the FSA is far too great to now seriously consider a global regulator.

7.97 There are two options: a single transnational regulator or domestic regulation but with increased co-operation through bodies such as IOSCO and FESCO. The development of a single regulator for the UK received almost unanimous support. Advantages include economies of scale; in real terms it is less expensive to operate a unitary system and since regulation costs are borne by the financial service markets, any reduction in indirect costs, over and above the actual costs of paying the regulator, should be welcomed.

7.98 Reporting requirements are centralised and unified, and this should have the effect of reducing the opportunities for duplication and improving efficiencies. Whilst there is no guarantee that a unitary regulator will possess all the range of diverse skills and expertise that exist under multiple regulators, the FSA has incorporated specialist divisions and areas of expertise.

7.99 Information sharing within and with external agencies is a priority for the FSA and a unified management structure will maximise the potential for ensuring effective communication and consistency of approach. The independent regulator cultures that pervaded under the former regime will gradually erode under the FSA as the strength of single authority decision-making is felt.

7.100 The advantages of economies of scale are not limited to the authority; there are also benefits for financial service providers as a single regulator should be efficient in dealing with suspected compliance irregularities, and matters would be resolved with the minimum of delay. This benefits consumers and will secure market confidence as well as providers, who will be subject to the minimum of disruption. In future market users can expect to see resources allocated to those areas of business that represent the highest risk. Under the single regulator model resources can be re-directed quickly and efficiently to deter any evolving risks and, in doing so, maintain consumer confidence.

7.101 The competing tensions that exist within the objectives of regulation across a diverse financial sector should be more easily resolved under one authority. It can be argued that the resolution of conflicts of interest is a matter for central government, assuming it has the expertise to deal with the issues; conversely, the powers vested in the FSA allow it to create rules and practices that should facilitate good practice and harmonisation of objectives. Whilst it is easy to see how this might have been hard to achieve with the establishment of individual regulators, who evolved over a lengthy period of time, one of the distinct advantages of a unitary system is that it has consistency.

7.102 Global unification of regulation is problematic and does not attract universal support. A number of industry professionals are of the view that adding any further layers of bureaucracy will simply impede entrepreneurship to the disadvantage of wealth creation. Second, market investors are rarely sophisticated and are highly vulnerable to local malpractice and criminal exploitation. This may be hard to address with a global model. Third, competition between regulators is not dysfunctional, as individual regulators will strive to achieve the best examples of regulation and, as such, attract greater domestic and international consumer confidence. Fourth, is it realistic to think that the USA will actually open its markets to Europe and other nation states? Perhaps not, as recent US banking legislation would indicate[1]. Perhaps the USA is more protective of national sovereignty than the EU; certainly the creation of a global regulator would challenge this and the principle that market governance is at the core of financial oversight.

---

1   Eg the Gramm, Leach, Bliley Financial Services Modernisation Act 1999, an Act that appears to create greater opportunities for US-based exchanges to compete for customers than it allows European capital markets.

7.103   Competitive inequalities are part of the agenda for domestic and international forums. The adoption of a single global regulator does not imply that there must be a 'one size fits all' approach. Different objectives and national interests can still be maintained, and should be encouraged, and appropriate differentiation is central to the activities of the FSA. This does not, however, negate the argument for unitary regulation that would achieve 'harmonisation, consolidation and rationalisation'[1].

1   For a detailed discussion on the merits of a single regulator for the UK see Briault, C, 'The Rationale for A Single National Financial Services Regulator', Occasional Papers Series (May 1999), FSA. The theme of 'Appropriate Differentiation' is discussed at p 22.

7.104   The establishment of financial conglomerates has enhanced the need for a global regulator. Just as these multinationals are adept at coping with complex multi-jurisdictional issues and a variety of applicable laws, so it must be possible that the existing regulators are capable of working together to overcome the legal and cultural barriers that exist to achieve one model of regulation. During the consultation and scrutiny stages of the FSMA 2000, concerns were expressed that the creation of a single regulator would create some form of draconian monster, 'a bureaucratic leviathan divorced from the industry it regulates'[1]. There is no simple way of averting concerns of this nature; it is accepted that they would be significantly magnified by the creation of a global regulator and, consequently, accountability must be at the forefront of any future convergence plans[2].

1   See Briault, C, 'The Rationale for A Single National Financial Services Regulator', Occasional Papers Series (May 1999), FSA. The theme of 'Appropriate Differentiation' is discussed at p 23.
2   For a brief, but salutary, warning that financial markets move faster than the political will to establish global regulation, see 'Don't wait for a global regulator', Editorial Comment, *The Nation*, 3 September 1999. Available at phuakl.tripod.com/pssm/archives.

7.105   As multi-national financial providers become commonplace, the financial service industry must accept that global multiple regulators may be increasingly ineffective in dealing with international financial emergencies. The UK is one example of the international move towards the development of a single national regulator. The formation of FESCO and IOSCO represent models that, for the present, seek to increase non-formal collaboration. The UK has accepted unitary regulation, it is currently evaluating a European Securities Commission. As national borders erode in a physical and virtual financial world, the establishment of an International Securities Commission can only be a matter of time.

Index

All references in this index are to paragraph numbers